SURVIVING THE WARMING

Strategies for Americans

Lorin R. Robinson, Ph.D.

Published by Open Books

Copyright © 2024 by Lorin R. Robinson

All rights reserved. No part of this book may be reproduced, scanned, or distributed in any printed or electronic form without permission except in the case of brief quotations embodied in critical articles and reviews.

Interior Design by Siva Ram Maganti

Cover image © by Chepko Danil Vitalevich shutterstock.com/g/chepko

Surviving the Warming: Strategies for Americans

A Review By
Diane Donovan
Senior Reviewer
Midwest Book Review

An excellent addition to books dealing with the political and scientific impact of the warming, but one that shows far more concern about the personal impact of living with the legacy that future generations will face.

While predicting that the warming will ultimately change civilization, the author provides strategies to help families construct themselves now and in future to adapt to the changed world—a source of strength that differentiates it from other books on the subject.

The warming will not only challenge where and how we live, but also make plain the importance of adopting reduced expectations and lifestyles stressing simplicity, self-reliance and sustainability.

From climate-driven migration, to changes in how and where food is grown, to employment outlooks, to the case for moving off-grid, Robinson considers not only how the warming happened, but assesses survival strategies individuals and families can use to respond to the crisis.

All this makes *Surviving the Warming* a powerful standout in climate change literature. It examines the world and society-wide changes to come and suggests how adults today can work with their kids and grandkids to cultivate the kinds of thinking and survival skills that will help assure a better quality of life as the warming warms. Its focus on multi-generational families highlights the need for immediate planning for the future.

The value of this approach is simply priceless, making *Surviving the Warming* a highly recommended must read for anyone interested in what the future may hold, and in helping their families, multi-generationally, to develop the skills to help assure their survival in the challenging world of the warming.

For Linda and Lucy

Contents

Foreword ... ix
Introduction ... xii
A Grim Glossary ... xvii

The Human Irony ... 1

Chapter 1: The Pandemic, Politics and Global Conflict ... 3
Chapter 2: Why Did We Take So Long to Get Worried? ... 9
Chapter 3: And Where Are We Going? ... 20

Survival of the Fittest ... 31

Chapter 1 "Tis a Gift to be Simple…" ... 33
Chapter 2 "Location, Location, Location!" ... 50
Chapter 3 Go North, Young Man, Go North ... 59
Chapter 4 Inflation and the Dismal Science ... 70
Chapter 5: Economic *Quid Quo Pro* ... 82
Chapter 6: America on the Move ... 92
Chapter 7: The Future of Food ... 99
Chapter 8: How Do We Feed Ourselves? ... 106
Chapter 9: "Whiskey's for Drinkin'; Water's for Fightin'!"* ... 118
Chapter 10: Keeping the Lights On ... 129
Chapter 11: Get Thee Off The Grid! ... 141
Chapter 12: Employment Opportunities ... 148
Chapter 13: Staying Healthy in a Warming World ... 160

Chapter 14: Safety and Security In The World of The Warming	169
Epilogue—"Earth Day" 2124	178
Appendix—Discussion Guide	186

FOREWORD

David M. Bird, Ph.D.
Emeritus Professor of Wildlife Biology
McGill University, Montreal

Wildlife biologists like me, who earned their doctorates in the seventies, tended to specialize in various taxonomic groups. Mine happens to be birds, raptorial species in particular, which, considering my surname, seems all too appropriate.

My name notwithstanding, I have always been fascinated by creatures sporting feathers and, in most cases, with an ability to fly. So, naturally, I'm concerned about their ongoing rapid extinction.

A recent study in *Science*, for example, points out that one in four birds—across species—has been lost in North America since 1950. Today, 12 percent of the world's roughly 10,500 bird species are in critical danger of extinction. And I am convinced that climate change is one of the major factors contributing to their demise.

Global warming, of course, is endangering not just our birds but all of the planet's species, including humankind. And what should be even more disturbing—Dr. Robinson, author of this timely book—strongly suggests that our situation is far worse than is being reported. His meticulous research clearly demonstrates that the laudable efforts to reduce greenhouse gas emissions will simply not be sufficient to save us entirely from the worst the warming will inevitably inflict upon us.

He provides many examples: Despite efforts to the contrary,

annual greenhouse gas emissions continue to increase every year. The total CO_2 emissions in 2023 were a record 37 billion tons. The forecast for 2024 is 37.5 billion tons.

Further, the parts-per-million concentration of CO_2 in the atmosphere now exceeds 425 ppm, well beyond the "tipping point" after which the adverse effects of the warming cannot be avoided. The last time the concentration of CO_2 reached 400+ ppm—some 3-4 million years ago—horses and camels lived in the high Arctic. Seas were at least 30-feet higher.

As the author points out, recent polling data indicates that as many as 80 percent of Americans now believe that the warming is real and that it presents a significant danger to future generations. But acceptance, he maintains, is only the first step. The question now becomes: What can individuals, families and extended families do to prepare to survive this ongoing civilization-changing climatic catastrophe?

His conclusion is that to survive the developing climate apocalypse, we will—today and for generations to come—need to adopt a survivalist outlook. We will need to adopt strategies and tools of survival and change our lifestyles in order to adapt. And this approach must be passed along from generation to generation.

The author maintains that the heat of the warming will "crack, blister and peel away what has always been the thin veneer of civilization," leading over time to the demise of civil society and the collapse of major institutions.

"Overall," he says, "we must be realistic and reduce our expectations in order to accept the warming's growing limitations. The mantra to use in developing viable lifestyles should be 'simplicity, self-reliance and sustainability'."

The book explores coming changes in housing, the economy, family finances, food, water, employment, energy, healthcare, safety and security, and the need for millions eventually to migrate away from increasingly inhospitable areas. It suggests ways in which families can prepare—starting now!

To encourage conversations about the need to prepare for the warming's inevitable impact, a detailed discussion guide is included to help organize urgently needed discussions about the seriousness of the situation and what can be done.

"My fear," Robinson says, "is that the frightening enormity of the monster we've created will lead to a paralyzing fatalism—the belief that nothing can be done to save us from its civilization-changing impact. But, as two million years of history have shown, humankind can be very flexible, adaptable and creative. Those are the traits that might be able to help us cope with what's coming."

Sad but true, this is a book whose time has more than come.

INTRODUCTION

"Success breeds excess;
A civilization falls
Under its own weight"
—Lorin R. Robinson

Congratulations! Since you're reading this, you are probably among those who have either dodged or discounted massive efforts by the anti-science radical right and the petrochemical, coal, and utility industries to discredit the science behind decades of warnings about the coming of Global Warming—or "the warming," as I choose to call it—and its serious consequences.

But accepting the reality of the warming is only a first step. We must now start preparing—as individuals, families and extended families—to survive the warming. My fear is that the frightening enormity of the monster we've created will lead to a paralyzing fatalism—the belief that nothing can be done to save us from its civilization changing impact.

One goal of this book is to disabuse readers of the idea that there's still hope that efforts to reduce greenhouse gas emissions will help us dodge the worst that the warming will bring, or that some technological trickery will yet come to the rescue. Section One lays those notions to rest.

Section Two, on the other hand, is devoted to what we can do to prepare to make the best of it. A series of thought exercises based on scientific realities considers basic needs such as housing, food, water, the economy, family finances, energy, employment, health, safety and security, the need for millions to migrate to less hostile climes and how, with planning starting *now*, we can increase the likelihood of survival.

The coming decades will require people to make many choices to help them confront challenges the warming is and will present. One of these will certainly be *how* we choose to live.

There is going to be the pressing need to readjust our expectations—our lifestyles— in order to cope with growing limitations imposed by the warming. There will be the need for people to accept—even embrace—simplicity, self-reliance and sustainability in how we organize our lives to survive in what will be a very different world. This will need to be a multi-generational effort.

While results of recent survey data, predictably, are mixed, it's evident that the majority of Americans have finally reached the conclusion that the warming is real and that it poses a significant threat to our civilization.

A recent study by The Yale Program on Climate Change Communication observed a dramatic increase in the share of Americans who are worried about climate change. The data indicated that over three-quarters of all voters (78 percent), including majorities of Democrats, Independents and Republicans, think that future generations will be seriously affected by the climate crisis.

However, according to *The Washington Post*, "even as windstorms became more powerful, wildfires grew more deadly and rising seas made damaging floods more frequent, Americans' views about the threat of global warming over the past few years remain largely unchanged." This according to a *Washington Post-ABC News* poll released early in 2022.

"A clear majority of adults say that warming is a serious problem, but the share—67 percent—is about the same as it was seven years ago."

The poll does find that the partisan divide over the issue has widened. The proportion of Democrats who see climate change as an existential threat has risen 11 points to 95 percent over the past seven years. Meanwhile, the share of Republicans who say climate change is a serious problem fell by 10 points, to 39 percent, over the same period.

The Republican decline in the Post-ABC poll tracks with the findings of annual Gallup polls in which Republicans' concerns dropped after 2017 when Donald Trump took office.

Chapter Two in Section One contains a detailed discussion about why *all* Americans—evidence to the contrary—aren't greatly concerned about the threat posed by the warming.

I am not a survivalist. I've always viewed survivalists as outliers living on the fringes of society—geographically and culturally—often seeking to disappear by living off-the-grid.

Their reasons are many and range from attempts to escape the soul-choking materialism of our society to finding freedom from government encroachment on what they perceive as personal freedoms. Other significant motivations include fear of domestic political unrest, nuclear holocaust and the escalating impact of warming-related climate events.

I thought survivalists were an interesting though relatively small demographic segment. Imagine my surprise on finding a survey indicating that, in a recent 12-month period, roughly 20 percent of Americans say they spent money on survival materials to prepare for "an apocalyptic doomsday."

It also appears the term "survivalist" has given way to "prepper." The latter is definitely not to be confused with "preppie." There are about a dozen magazines and numerous websites and blogs that cover all aspects of survivalism.

A survivalist/prepper is someone who prepares for possible dangers by stockpiling necessary supplies and acquiring survival skills. The emphasis is on self-reliance and self-sufficiency. Survivalists often acquire emergency medical and self-defense training and build survival retreats or underground shelters that may help them survive a catastrophe.

Survivalists/preppers may be found within all demographic strata of society—including the super-rich. While most of the rest of us are just starting to think about how we can prepare to deal with the warming, many of the "One" and ".01" Percenters are already actively planning for their futures and the futures of their offspring in the dystopian world that's likely to come.

We should not, as I had, view preppers as kooks in tin foil hats sitting around awaiting the end of times. In many ways, and for whatever their reasons, they are pioneers. The general population will have a lot to learn from them as the climate crisis rolls into gear in the coming years and decades.

As indicated, it is a central thesis of this book that, to survive the developing climate apocalypse, we will—as individuals, families, and extended families for generations to come—need to adopt a survivalist outlook; to adopt and adapt strategies and tools of survival. These strategies and others are the focus of Section Two of this survival manual.

Most readers like to know what kind of book it is they're reading. Usually, a book is simple to identify. It's either fiction or non-fiction and falls into one of the many specific genres. Not so with this book.

I like to think of it largely as non-fiction since it's based on current research by the climate and earth sciences. But, since the book looks ahead into a very murky future, much of it is speculation—by me and by others. It's a hybrid.

I cannot claim credentials as a scientist or futurist. I'm the kind of guy who has trouble balancing his checkbook. Nor can I claim to be unusually adept at prognostication. Almost everything going on around me comes as a surprise.

What I can claim, however, is a long career in journalism and journalism education and an intense decade-long interest in the warming. The research I've done led to two climate fiction books on the subject—*The Warming* (2015) and *Tales from The Warming* (2017). Though fiction, both books were scrupulously based on the findings of science. They were efforts to extrapolate from the data to imagine the impact of the warming on people—around the world and over time.

In short, they were thought exercises.

So, instead of predictions or prognostications, *Surviving The Warming* is a series of thought exercises that consider *possibilities*. It suggests the personal, social, economic, political and environmental challenges our planet's human inhabitants will face multi-generationally and how we can best begin to prepare to survive them.

My hope is that this book will encourage conversations about the need to start preparing for the warming's inevitable impact. A discussion guide provided as an appendix is designed to provide the reader with a summary of key information drawn from the book. This material can be used to structure a discussion about the seriousness of the situation and what can be done to make the best of the difficult times to come.

A GRIM GLOSSARY

A number of terms and concepts will turn up in the book that follows. Though they will be defined in context as necessary, here's a running start at some of the key terminology to come. There will not be a test.

Albedo—The fraction of light reflected by a body or surface, commonly used in astronomy to describe the reflective properties of planets, satellites and asteroids. Increases in global temperature cause snow and ice to melt, which decreases Earth's albedo. This decrease means more energy is absorbed, which causes further warming that in turn causes more melting.

Alternative Energy Sources—There are six widely-available non-fossil fuel sources of energy that have been available for decades—in one case for over 100 years. They are solar, wind, nuclear, hydro, thermal and tidal. As of this writing, less than 30 percent of the world's energy is provided by non-fossil fuels.

Anthropogenic Extinction—The extinction of species due to human activities, otherwise referred to as the "Sixth Extinction." It is ongoing and taking place during the present Holocene Epoch (since around 10,000 BCE). Throughout the 4.6 billion years of Earth's history, there have been five other major mass extinction events that each wiped out an overwhelming majority of species living at the time.

Bomb Cyclone—Warming ocean waters create ideal conditions for "bomb cyclone" events formed by air close to the surface rising rapidly, causing barometric pressure to plunge—an effect known as "bombogenesis." The low-pressure area sucks in frigid air, often then delivered to land by a sagging jet stream and resulting in intense rain and/or snow, hurricane force winds and flooding. The North Atlantic states are particularly vulnerable.

CO_2 PPM—*The parts-per-million concentration of CO_2 in the atmosphere now exceeds the 425 ppm, well beyond the "tipping point" after which the adverse effects of the warming cannot be avoided.* The last time the concentration of CO_2 reached 400+ ppm—some 3-4 million years ago—horses and camels lived in the high Arctic. Seas were at least 30-feet higher—a level that today would inundate major coastal cities around the world—and the planet was an average of 3.6-6.2°F (2-4°C) warmer.

Drought—A period when an area or region experiences below-normal precipitation—either rain or snow—that can reduce soil moisture or groundwater, diminish stream flow, damage crops, cause a general water shortage and desertification. At the peak of the 2012 drought in the U.S.—the most extensive since the 1930s—an astounding 81 percent of the country was ranked as under at least abnormally dry conditions.

Ecocide—Destruction of the natural environment by deliberate or negligent human action, suggesting that no one should go unpunished for destroying the natural world. Supporters believe the crime should come under the jurisdiction of the International Criminal Court, which can currently prosecute four crimes: genocide, war crimes, crimes of aggression and *crimes against humanity*.

El Ninõ and La Ninã—El Niño means "the little boy" in Spanish and La Niña, "the little girl." They are opposite phases of a temperature variation between the ocean and the atmosphere over the east-central tropical Pacific. These phases usually occur once every few years and last nine to 12 months but can sometimes last years. During an El Niño event, the east to west trade winds die, keeping the normal air in the tropical Pacific warmer, resulting in warmer water and more stormy weather around the Americas. La Niña is essentially the opposite of El Niño. Trade winds strengthen. The eastern and central parts of the tropical Pacific become colder, while the west is warmer and experiences more rainfall.

Frankenstorms—A term applied to mega-hurricanes. Sandy in 2012 earned the nickname "Frankenstorm" since it wreaked havoc in 24 states on its march from the central Caribbean, across Jamaica, Cuba and the Bahamas and up the Eastern seaboard. The highest storm surge in New York City was measured at the tip of Manhattan—14 feet. The resulting flooding knocked out the subway system and closed all but one tunnel entering Manhattan. The storm killed 285 and caused an estimated $75 billion in damages.

Global Mean Temperature Increase—The current worst-case average planetary temperature forecast increase for 2100 is 9.7°F (6°C) above the 1900 baseline. But remember that this is an average increase. The farther south one goes in the Northern Hemisphere or north in the Southern Hemisphere, the higher the temperatures will range above the average. The Tropic of Cancer circles the Earth at approximately 23.5° north of the equator—the northernmost point where the sun's rays can appear directly overhead at local noon. Its southern counterpart is the Tropic of Capricorn. The area between this 5,000-plus mile wide band circling the center of the planet will suffer most from increasing temperatures. The increasing temperatures, of course, will result in increasing drought and desertification in the U.S. and around the planet as well as mass migrations of humans either to the north or south.

Greenhouse Gas Pollution (GHG)—During the early years of the Industrial Revolution, French scientist Joseph Fourier proposed that energy reaching the planet as sunlight must be balanced by energy returning to space since heated surfaces emit radiation.

But some of that energy, he reasoned, must be held within the atmosphere, keeping the Earth warm.

He proposed that the planet's atmosphere acts the way a glass greenhouse would; the more GHG there is, the more energy is kept within the atmosphere. Irish scientist John Tyndall in the 1860s showed that coal gas (containing CO_2, methane and volatile hydrocarbons) was especially effective at absorbing energy. He demonstrated that CO_2 alone acts like sponge, absorbing multiple wavelengths of sunlight. *Global carbon dioxide emissions from fossil fuels totaled 37 billion tons in 2023. Emissions are projected rise to 1.1 percent in 2024 to a record high of 37.5 tons.*

Gulf Stream—One of Earth's major climate-regulating ocean currents (i.e. Ocean Conveyor Belt), the Gulf Stream is moving slower than it has in thousands of years. Several studies show that this slowdown increases sea-level rise on the U.S. coast for cities like New York and Boston. Other studies link heat waves and severe storms (bomb cyclones) in the eastern United States to the weakened current. The primary cause of the disruption appears to be the trillions of tons of fresh water flowing continuously off the Greenland glacier.

Habitable Niche—Areas where humans have historically lived due to favorable temperature and precipitation. For the past 6,000 years, humans have mostly lived in the same climate conditions as they do now. This climate niche is also where production of crops and livestock typically take place. The optimal mean annual temperature of this identified niche is 52° – 59°F (11° – 15°C). But, as the climate changes, the areas that fit within the human climate niche are becoming smaller. Currently only 0.8 percent of the global land surface has a mean annual temperature greater than 84°F (29°C), but, by 2070, breathtakingly hot temperatures are projected to cover 19 percent of the world and affect an estimated 3.5 billion people.

Methane (CH)—The second most abundant GHG after carbon

dioxide, accounting for 12 percent of global emissions. But it's more than 28 times as effective in trapping heat in the atmosphere. Methane is emitted during the production and transport of coal, natural gas, oil and fracking. Its emissions also result from livestock and other agricultural practices, land use, and by the decay of organic waste in municipal solid waste landfills.

Mitigation vs. Adaptation—Now that the world, finally, has become concerned about the impact of the warming, efforts are being directed mainly at curbing GHG emissions—called "mitigation." As will be seen, however, these efforts will not save the planet and its inhabitants from the wrath of the warming. What's needed now—and what this book is about—are concerted efforts at "adaptation" (survival). What we need to deal as effectively as possible with the coming dystopia—as individuals, families, communities, states and the nation—is to develop viable adaptive strategies.

National Oceanic and Atmospheric Administration—Referred to as NOAA in the text.

Ocean acidification—Called by some "Global Warming's Evil Twin," ocean acidification is doing to the seas what the warming is doing to the land—gradually making it less habitable, in this case, for marine life. The term refers to an increase in the acidity of the ocean over an extended period of time caused primarily by absorption of CO_2 from the atmosphere. When carbon dioxide dissolves into seawater, it forms carbonic acid (H_2CO_3). The ocean absorbs about 30 percent of the CO2 released in the atmosphere. At the current rate of absorption, it's estimated that by 2100 the seas will be 150 times more acidic than they are today. Much aquatic life will simply not have time to adapt, likely resulting in a mass die off over time up and down the food chain.

Outgassing tundra—When it comes to predicting the course of the warming, unanticipated consequences play a major role. A recent discovery explains, in part, why the climate crisis seems to be accelerating faster than had been forecast. Huge quantities of CO_2 and methane gases are being released by the rapidly melting Arctic and Siberian tundra. *It's estimated four times as much CO_2 is locked in the tundra than has ever been emitted by humans.* This phenomenon had not been considered in earlier modeling.

Polar Vortex—An area of low pressure parked in the arctic polar region—a wide expanse of cold air swirling counter-clockwise. During winter, the vortex expands, sending cold air southward, often in conjunction with a sagging jet stream. This happens fairly often and can be associated with outbreaks of cold temperatures in the U.S. More recently, the vortex, in conjunction with the jet stream, moved low enough to collide with hot, humid air from The Gulf of Mexico resulting in dangerous fronts producing out-of-season tornado outbreaks and damaging thunderstorm activity in multiple states.

Sea-level Rise (SLR)—Often referred to in the text as SLR for brevity's sake. SLR, of course, is one the most dangerous outcomes of the warming. Since the 1900 benchmark, the seas, on average, have risen about one foot. SLR is increasing more rapidly as warmer temperatures melt ice caps and glaciers around the planet. Worldwide, based on data available in 2017, NOAA predicts a worst-case sea-level increase of approximately three feet by 2050, sufficient to inundate many major coastal cities. NOAA's nightmare scenario for 2100—over eight feet.

SHTF Event—An acronym that stands for a "Shit Hits the Fan" event, one that is extremely disruptive to the social order. Preppers (survivalists) use the term to describe a situation in which government efforts to contain a situation either do no good or make things worse and one in which people are no longer guaranteed the ability to obtain survival necessities like food, water and shelter. An SHTF Event is extraordinarily disruptive to day-to-day living and likely to result in panic and violence.

Storm Surge—One of the most dangerous features of hurricanes, storm surges are the abnormal rise in seawater level during a storm measured as the height of the water above the normal predicted astronomical tide. A surge is caused primarily by a storm's winds pushing water onshore. In the U.S., one of the greatest recorded storm surges was generated by Hurricane Katrina in 2005—nearly 28 feet—flattening 90 percent of the structures in Pass Christian, MS.

Survivalist/Prepper—Someone who prepares for possible dangers by stockpiling necessary supplies and acquiring survival skills. The emphasis is on self-reliance and self-sufficiency. Survivalists often acquire emergency medical and self-defense training and/or build survival retreats or underground shelters that may help them survive a catastrophe. In a recent survey, 20 percent of Americans said they bought survival materials to prepare for "an apocalyptic doomsday."

The Warming—My first book was called The Warming (2015). I may have coined the term. Obviously, the phenomenon is global in nature. So, the word "global" seems unnecessary. You may also notice that I use the term "climate change" only when quoting others. The phrase was invented by warming deniers to make it easier to place the blame elsewhere. The warming is the cause; "climate change" is an effect.

United Nations Framework Convention on Climate Change (UNFCCC)—The first international conference of the UNFCCC—an unfortunate mouthful—was held in Berlin in 1995. What followed were annual meetings around the world characterized by the inability to reach consensus on meaningful measures to reign in GHG pollution. There also developed an understandable schism between developed/industrialized nations and the so-called "Third World" with developing nations blaming "First World" countries for causing the problem.

UN Global Climate Fund (GCF)—At the 2009 UN climate talks, developing countries were promised substantial help to kick the fossil-fuel habit while they worked to develop economically. Funds from first-world taxpayers and the private sector were to be placed in an UN-administered climate fund. Developed countries promised to provide $100 billion a year by 2020 from a variety of sources. As of October, 2020, *only $10.3 billion* had been pledged to the fund.

Wet Bulb Temperature—Increasing heat alone won't determine the world's fate. A new climate analysis explains how, when humidity and heat collide, they create "wet bulb" temperatures that will disrupt daily existence. When heat meets excessive humidity, the body can no longer cool itself by sweating. High wet bulb temperatures make it dangerous to work and play outdoors. As wet bulb temperatures increase, so does the risk of heat stroke—and even death.

Section One
The Human Irony

"During the 4.6 billion years of the planet's history, it has undergone unbelievable transformations based on changes in its axis or orbit around the sun. At one time Earth has been an ice world, a water world, a desert world, a fiery Hell. It's inhabitants have also been the victims of cataclysmic events—five of them—that nearly wiped all living organisms from its surface. The most recent was our collision with an asteroid the size of the Empire State Building. Dinosaurs had reigned then—66 million years ago. Their demise opened a niche for the small mammals who survived—our ancestors. Now it seems we are entering a sixth extinction—one that is human caused."

—Lorin R. Robinson

Chapter One

The Pandemic, Politics and Global Conflict

"This pandemic has magnified every existing inequality in our society—like systemic racism, gender inequality and poverty."
—Melinda Gates

"Trump only cares how the covid-19 pandemic affects him, his bank account, and his chances of getting re-elected."
—Oliver Markus Malloy

The warming is looming on the horizon like the thick orange smoke from wildfires crisping vast swaths of our western states. But, recently, of necessity, the world shifted attention to a large extent from the growing global climate crisis to dealing with a global pandemic and increasing global conflict.

As of this writing, over seven million deaths from COVID-19 have been reported globally. In the United States, supposedly one of the world's most technologically and medically advanced nations, the toll is more than 1.2 million and—despite the availability of vaccines—still rising.

Simple math indicates the U.S., with just over four percent of the world's population, has suffered more than 17 percent of the deaths. The reason is well known and not the subject of this book, but, for the record, the criminal mismanagement or lack of management by Donald Trump and his inept administration is largely responsible. Sharing the blame more recently is the large contingent (about 30 percent) of the population that is anti-science, anti-vaccine.

But it's not just the pandemic that's diverting peoples' attention from the warming. In the U.S., a majority of the population is concerned about efforts to blow up democracy through enactment of voter suppression laws, politicization of the election process and harassment of non-partisan election officials and workers—all in support of former President Trump's unfounded "big lie" about fraud in the 2020 election.

This concern extends to Trump and his allies regaining control of both Houses of Congress and the White House, thus ensuring a return to policies detrimental to the environment and to taking necessary steps to slow and prepare for the warming. One of his first actions in office in 2017 was to renege on U.S. commitments made at the Paris climate summit in 2015. He also ordered his Environmental "Destruction" Agency to roll back or eliminate all policies in place to curb U.S. greenhouse gas emissions (GHG).

There is a significant lesson to be learned here about the need for strong, centralized and empathetic political leadership in order to deal, not only with a pandemic and the threat to free and fair elections, but with the coming civilization-changing effects of the warming as well. To try to minimize the impact of what is rapidly developing as a global catastrophe of epic proportions, our country—the so-called "leader of the free world"—will need to do a significantly better job of dealing with the warming than it did with the pandemic.

The dramatic increase in global conflict in recent decades is also a major cause of concern. The warming is a global issue, but how can the world deal with it effectively when also facing geo-political turmoil?

A dangerous mix of increasing international conflict, global climate change, and a lack of governmental efforts to fix either could be leading the world to an era of unprecedented destruction.

That's the thrust of a 2022 report from Stockholm International Peace Institute (SIPRI).

The report is titled "Environment of Peace," a hopeful title that belies the report's horrifying message: The twin dangers of conflict—meaning wars or violence between or within countries and climate change—are interconnected and getting worse.

The report paints a vivid picture of the escalating security crisis. According to the Institute, "Between 2010 and 2020 the number of state-based armed conflicts roughly doubled to 56, as did the number of conflict-related deaths. The number of refugees and other forcibly displaced people also doubled to 82.4 million. In 2020 the number of operationally deployed nuclear warheads increased after years of reductions, and in 2021 military spending surpassed $2 trillion for the first time ever."

It rose to $2.25 trillion in 2023.

Global conflict dropped dramatically after the fall of the Soviet Union in 1991. But, as the report noted, that trend reversed in 2010.

"Even before the Russian invasion of Ukraine, geopolitics was becoming discernibly more fraught," the report said. "A particular feature has been the increasingly frosty relationship between China and several Western powers, notably the United States."

The alarming rise in authoritarian leadership and ultra-nationalism around the world, should it continue apace, will also certainly make efforts to deal with the warming on a global level considerably more difficult.

According to a recent report by the International Red Cross, the world should react with the same urgency to the climate crisis as to the coronavirus virus, warning that the warming poses a greater threat than COVID-19.

Even as the pandemic raged, the warming wreaked evermore death and destruction around the planet and in the U.S.

Part of the scorecard since 2020:

- NOAA reports that 2021 was one of the most catastrophic climate years on record—688 people died and about $145 billion was lost in the U.S. as a result of extreme weather events associated with the warming. And 2022 was also deadly with weather events causing at least 474 deaths. Damages from the 2022 disasters totaled $165.1 billion.

- Hurricane Ida in 2021 killed 95 and was the fourth-costliest hurricane in U.S. history, causing at least $100 billion in uninsured and insured damage. But a year later, Hurricane Ian killed at least 156 and caused more than $112 billion in damage, most coming in Florida ($109.5 billion). That makes it the costliest hurricane in Florida history and the third costliest in the U.S. behind Katrina (2005) and Harvey (2017).

- A massive out-of-season tornado outbreak in December, 2021 flattened cities and killed nearly 100 in five states.

- The wildfire season in the West was the worst on record in 2021, destroying as much acreage as the State of New Hampshire. Wildfires in 2022 consumed over 7.5 million acres of wildland.

- 2023 was the warmest year by a wide margin since global records began in 1850. It was 2.12°F (1.18°C) above the twentieth-century average of 57.0°F (13.9°C).

- In 2023, the U.S. experienced 28 separate weather and climate disasters each costing at least one billion dollars; the highest number of billion-dollar disasters in a calendar year.

For some perspective on climate-related damage, consider that the failed Biden Build Back Better Bill included only $555 billion to tackle the warming *over the next 10 years*. That's a mere $55 billion a year. The cleanup following Hurricane Ian alone was an estimated $112 billion.

As an alternative, the Biden administration was able to push through the Inflation Reduction Act (IRA) in August, 2022. The IRA includes a host of programs aimed at addressing climate change and energy production, including $369 billion to encourage the reduction of GHG. The IRA also included dozens of new and extended tax credits for renewable energy, electric vehicles, electric transmission, and related industries.

Although the most aggressive climate initiative ever approved, it fell almost $200 billion short of climate-earmarked funds in the BBB bill. Still, the administration claims the package will curb the country's carbon emissions by a very optimistic 40 percent by 2030.

At the 2015 Paris climate talks, the U.S. had committed to reduce its GHG emissions by 26-28 percent below the 2005 level by 2025, which has turned out to be unrealistic. In the intervening four years, the Trump administration put the brakes on, threatening to withdraw our commitment.

In any case, both initiatives were earmarked primarily for "mitigation"—converting Federal government vehicles to electric, for example. But, while GHG reduction is a worthwhile effort, it should not be the only focus. People and the economy are already being challenged to deal with the misery, damage and destruction wrought by the warming, thus requiring increased efforts aimed at "adaptation."

And there's more bad news. A recent discovery explains, in part, why the climate crisis seems to be accelerating faster than had been forecast. Huge quantities of CO_2 and methane gases are being released by the rapidly melting Arctic and Siberian tundra. It's estimated that four times as much CO_2 is locked in the tundra than has ever been emitted by humans. This phenomenon had not been considered in earlier modeling.

For reasons not yet fully understood, the Arctic Region is warming approximately twice as fast as the rest of the world. It's possible that, as the Arctic Ocean rapidly melts, the region's albedo (reflectivity) is reduced. Thus, the dark waters beneath the disappearing ice are absorbing ever more solar energy.

A cynic might suggest that this massive outgassing is a form of planetary revenge.

While it's not possible to stop the warming's onslaught, it's still possible to blunt its impact to some extent through significant and immediate reduction of GHG emissions. But the fact is that the warming is already "baked in." We are literally at the point of no return—not a tipping point. We've already tipped.

As of this writing, there are 425 ppm of CO_2 in the atmosphere. The last time the concentration of Earth's greenhouse gases reached 400+ ppm—some 3-4 million years ago—horses and camels lived in the high Arctic. Seas were at least 30-feet higher—a level that today would inundate major coastal cities around the world—and the planet was an average of 3.6-6.2°F (2-4°C) warmer.

Meanwhile we continue to pump an estimated 37 billion tons of CO_2 into our skies annually. And a chemist will tell you that the CO_2 molecule is very robust, taking up *to 90 years to decompose in* the atmosphere.

Attention being paid to the warming these days focuses primarily on the macro level—the big picture—as climate scientists chart global temperature increases, measure the rising oceans, study the changing weather patterns, drought and the loss of viable agricultural lands. That's relatively easy.

What's not as easy is to bring the looming disaster down to the micro level. What is and will be the impact of these worldwide phenomena on people—you, me, our families today and on future generations?

The billions wrung from the U.S. economy to soften the economic and social impact of the pandemic will pale in comparison to the enormous sums required to keep the nation functioning in the face of the rising oceans, drought and increasingly violent weather.

Chapter Two
Why Did We Take So Long to Get Worried?

"The furnaces of the world are now burning about two billion tons of coal a year. When this is burned, uniting with oxygen, it adds about seven billion tons of carbon dioxide to the atmosphere yearly. This tends to make the air a more effective blanket for the earth and to raise its temperature. The effect may be considerable in a few centuries." —Rodney and Otamatea Times, New Zealand, August 14, 1912, under the headline "Coal Consumption Affecting Climate."

"The Arctic Ocean is warming up, icebergs are growing scarcer and, in some places, the seals are finding the water too hot....

"Reports from fishermen, seal hunters and explorers all point to a radical change in climate conditions and hitherto unheard-of temperatures in the Arctic zone. Exploration expeditions report that scarcely any ice has been met as far north as 81 degrees 29 minutes.... Great masses of ice have been replaced by moraines of earth and stones...while at many points well-known glaciers have entirely disappeared.

"Very few seals and no white fish are found in the eastern Arctic, while vast shoals of herring and smelt, which have never before ventured so far north, are being encountered in the old seal fishing grounds." —Washington Post, November 2, 1922

We haven't lacked for early warnings.

In the 1820s, during the early years of the Industrial Revolution, French mathematician and physicist Joseph Fourier proposed that energy reaching the planet as sunlight must be balanced by energy returning to space since heated surfaces emit radiation. But some of that energy, he reasoned, must be held within the atmosphere, keeping the Earth warm.

He proposed that the planet's thin atmosphere acts the way a glass greenhouse does. Energy enters through the glass walls but is then trapped inside. Much like a warm greenhouse—the more GHG there are, the more energy is kept within the atmosphere.

The greenhouse effect analogy stuck and, some 40 years later, Irish scientist John Tyndall explored exactly what kinds of gases were most likely to play a role in absorbing sunlight.

Tyndall's laboratory tests in the 1860s showed that coal gas—containing CO_2, methane and volatile hydrocarbons—was especially effective at absorbing energy. He eventually demonstrated that CO_2 alone acted like sponge in the way it absorbed multiple wavelengths of sunlight.

By 1895, Swedish chemist Svante Arrhenius, in order to explain past ice ages, was curious about how decreasing levels of CO_2 in the atmosphere might cool Earth. He wondered if a decrease in volcanic activity might lower global CO_2 levels. His calculations showed that if CO_2 levels were halved, global average temperatures could decrease by about 9°F (5°C).

Next, Arrhenius wondered if the reverse were true. He returned to his calculations, this time asking what would happen if CO_2 levels were doubled. The possibility seemed remote at the time, but his results suggested that global temperatures would increase by the same amount.

Decades later, modern climate modeling has confirmed that Arrhenius's numbers weren't far off the mark.

More recently, a Columbia University professor and researcher brought the term "global warming" into common use.

Wallace Smith Broecker used the phrase in a 1975 article

correctly predicting that rising carbon dioxide levels in the atmosphere would lead to pronounced warming. He later became the first person to recognize what he called the "Ocean Conveyor Belt," a global network of currents affecting everything from air and water temperature to rain patterns.

In 1984, Broecker told a congressional subcommittee that the buildup of GHG warranted a "bold, new national effort aimed at understanding the operation of the realms of the atmosphere, oceans, ice and terrestrial biosphere."

"We live in a climate system that can jump abruptly from one state to another," Broecker told the Associated Press in 1997. "By dumping into the atmosphere huge amounts of GHG, such as carbon dioxide from the burning of fossil fuels, we are conducting an experiment that could have devastating effects."

What followed was recognition by the UN that it had a responsibility to encourage and support further research on what was now widely being called "global warming," and to provide an international forum for gaining consensus on solutions to deal with what was seen as a rapidly developing and significant problem.

The first international conference of the United Nations Framework Convention on Climate Change (UNFCCC)—an unfortunate mouthful—was held in Berlin in 1995. What followed were annual meetings around the world characterized by the inability to reach consensus on meaningful measures to reign in GHG pollution. There also developed an understandable schism between industrialized nations and the so-called Third World.

Developing nations, naturally, were reluctant to promise to curb their use of the cheap fossil fuels with which they were building their economies. The warming puts poorer nations in a double bind. They are being asked to cut emissions by converting to alternative energies. But, without economic growth coming from burning cheap fossil fuels, they cannot afford conversion to non-fossil fuels, nor can they afford costly cleanup efforts necessary to deal with the growing crisis.

They rightly blamed the industrial world for polluting the atmosphere. At the moment, the top five polluters—China, the U.S., the European Union, India, Russia—contribute over 60 percent of the world's CO_2 emissions.

At the 2009 UN climate talks in Copenhagen—to try to heal the rift—poor countries were promised substantial help to kick the fossil-fuel habit while they worked to develop economically. Funds from first-world taxpayers and the private sector were to be placed in a UN Green Climate Fund (GCF). Developed countries promised to provide $30 billion for the period 2010-2012 and to mobilize long-term financing for a further $100 billion a year by 2020 from a variety of sources.

And how is the First World doing with that pledge? As of October, 2020, a total of *only $10.3 billion had been pledged to the fund.*

Perhaps the most heralded and hopeful of the UN Climate Conferences took place in Paris in 2015. The aim of the conference was, finally, to reach a binding agreement to control the warming by stabilizing atmospheric concentrations of GHG. At that point the UNFCCC had 195 members. The conference led to the Paris Agreement that was later adopted and ratified by 174 countries.

Prior to the conference, *National Geographic* cast this pessimistic note: "Since 1992, when the world's nations agreed at Rio de Janeiro to avoid dangerous anthropogenic interference with the climate system, they've met 20 times without moving the needle on carbon emissions. In that interval we've added almost as much carbon to the atmosphere as we did in the previous century."

The ultimate goal of the convention was to reduce emissions of GHG in order to allow no more than a 3.6°F (2°C) rise in the average global temperature above pre-industrial levels. This, it was believed, would allow the world to dodge some of the worst that the warming has to offer. Countries were required to outline measures they would take to reduce their GHG emissions. The result was a binding agreement on emission reduction, the first in the 20 years of UN climate conferences.

The conference was not, however, without controversy.

In a joint letter, some of the world's top climate scientists launched a blistering attack on the deal, warning that it offers "false hope" that could ultimately prove to be counterproductive in the battle to curb global warming. The scientists claimed that the measures agreed upon were too weak and did not do enough to reduce emissions of GHG.

They pointed out that in as early as the third page of the draft agreement is the acknowledgment that targeted CO_2 reductions won't keep the global temperate rise below 3.6°F (2°C), the level that was set as the critical limit.

Developing nations also voiced their disappointment over lack of support for the financial plan (the GCF) that was to compensate those countries affected by global warming.

Why, after all the early and more strident recent warnings, do we find ourselves hurtling toward a global climate catastrophe like a runaway train running out of track?

One explanation may be found in the uncounted millions in advertising, public relations, support of pseudoscience and lobbying spent by the energy industries and right-wing warming deniers in an effort to convince the public that the warming wasn't real. Failing that, their focus shifted to blaming a "natural warming cycle" as the culprit. Failing that, we were told that forecast negative effects are exaggerated.

This campaign of outright lies and disinformation is reminiscent of that perpetrated by the tobacco industry in its successful 50-year defense of smoking. It's the same playbook. Only, in this case, the deceit has been far more harmful. It has misled and confused the public, substantially slowing society's reaction to this potentially civilization-changing crisis.

Senator Throws Snowball! Climate Change Disproven!

Sen. James Inhofe (R-Oklahoma) was one of Congress's most ardent global warming deniers. He also hails from Oklahoma, a state whose economy and politics are controlled by the petrochemical industry—the source for much of his campaign funding.

The highlight of Inhofe's otherwise undistinguished tenure in the Senate was to throw a snowball in the Senate chambers to draw attention to unseasonably cold weather in February, 2015 in Washington D.C.

The Senator, author of the book *The Greatest Hoax*, has made something of a cottage industry out of arguing that climate change is "the greatest hoax ever perpetrated on the American people." At last, he had proof that he'd been right all along.

Inhofe brought his snowball onto the floor of the Senate on February 26, 2015 and declared that "we keep hearing that 2014 has been the warmest year on record." Yet in a plastic bag, right on his desk, he had the evidence to demolish that claim. "I ask the chair; you know what this is? It's a snowball, and that's just from outside here, so it's very, very cold out, very unseasonable." Then he tossed the unexpected snowball to the unsuspecting chair.

Inhofe was correct, of course. It was unseasonably cold. But it was also very unseasonably hot in Opa-Locka, Florida, that same day where the temperature was a record-breaking 87°F—sweltering even for that part of the country that time of year. Presumably, Opa-Locka's unseasonable steam bath is equally compelling proof to the contrary—that climate change is real.

For a detailed account of deniers' unfounded attacks on climate science and scientists, read Michael Mann's *The Hockey Stick and the Climate Wars* (2012).

"Public discourse has been polluted now for decades by corporate-funded disinformation—not just with climate change but with a host of health, environmental and societal threats. The implications for the planet are grim," according to Mann.

This kind of corporate and political misbehavior that disregards the future of the human race has led many, from the Pope to young activist Greta Thunberg, to call for the crime of "ecocide" to be recognized in international criminal law.

Ecocide—which literally means "killing the environment"—is an idea that seems radical but, supporters claim, is a reasonable one. The theory is that no one should go unpunished for destroying the natural world. Campaigners believe the crime should come under the jurisdiction of the International Criminal Court, which can currently prosecute four crimes: genocide, war crimes, crimes of aggression and *crimes against humanity.*

While it is unlikely that petrochemical, coal or utility chief executives will see the insides of jail cells, there are many who believe they should. Others in the U.S. believe certain government officials are equally culpable.

Alaska Governor Solves Funding Crisis for Climate Cleanup

Alaska's Gov. Bill Walker had an interesting idea about how to fund cleanup of his state's growing climate change problem. He requested in 2015 that the Obama Administration allow his state to authorize more oil drilling.

In an interview with the BBC's Matt McGrath, the Alaska Governor said:

> *"We are in a significant fiscal challenge. We have villages that are washing away because of the change in the climate. Relocating these villages is proving to be very expensive."*

McGrath pressed: "So you're saying that, given the climate change impacts in Alaska, you need to be allowed to continue to drill and explore and produce oil to pay for some of those impacts?"

Walker's response: "Absolutely."

Later McGrath would later comment: "That's just about the most remarkable statement I've ever encountered."

Taking an active and rational approach to the warming was dealt another major blow with the election of Donald Trump in 2016. His position on the warming may best be summed up by one of his incessant tweets: "The concept of global warming was created by and for the Chinese in order to make U.S. manufacturing non-competitive."

According to fact checkers who kept close track, that's just another of the more than 30,000 lies he told to the American public during his four-year term.

Former President Trump vowed to dismantle the U.S. commitment to the 2015 Paris climate accord, signaling his desire for America not to cooperate with global efforts to rein in GHG pollution. And, as indicated, he exhorted the EPA to delete any vestiges of earlier regulations to deal with the crisis.

Trump, like most Republicans, slavishly adheres to the notion that efforts to minimize the effects of the warming will require more "big government" and cause serious injury to our vaunted and largely mythical system of "free enterprise." He and his minions applied the same rationale to dealing—or not dealing—with the pandemic. He famously told the country: "It's up to the states," implying that the pandemic is a local and not a national problem.

Fortunately, Trump and his enablers were routed from the White House in 2020. The Biden Administration appears to be making the warming a top priority—along with undoing all the other damage and potential damage to the country and our democracy wrought by its previous inhabitant.

President Biden's orders cover domestic and international matters, including cancelling Trump's withdrawal from the World Health Organization and rejoining the Paris climate accord.

Rejoining the Paris pact was only a first step in Biden's broad efforts to elevate the climate crisis to among his administration's top priorities. He ordered executive agencies to review 103 Trump-era actions on the environment and public health, a potential wholesale reversal of his efforts to deregulate in ways that helped fossil-fuel companies and other sectors of heavy industry.

How well the Biden Administration does in the short term in implementing programs to slow our GHG emissions, of course, depends on who controls both houses of Congress and sits in the White House after 2024.

In case there's anymore that needs to be said about how politics influences environmental policy....

The Grinch Who Stole Build Back Better*
December 24, 2021
by Lorin Robinson
*Excerpts from an opinion column,
Madison (WI) Capital-Times

Sen. Joe Manchin has been called lots of things—including the well-deserved "DINO" (Democrat in Name Only).

In single-handedly scuttling President Biden's Build Back Better agenda, DINO Manchin not only disrespected the wishes of his own party and President, but that of the public as well. Depending on what poll one reads, 60-70 percent of Americans strongly supported all or most of the Biden Bill—including many Republicans.

Another label that comes to mind on this Christmas Eve is "Grinch." Only, in this case, this Grinch did not steal "jing-tinglers," "floofloovers" and "tartookas" from kids in Whoville. He stuffed much needed social, medical and environmental programs up the chimney.

Among environmentally related programs is the $555 billion for renewable energy and clean transportation.

Biden's "socialist" agenda has, of course, resulted in frenzied corporate lobbying—particularly from the fossil-fuel and medical-insurance industries—the likes of which Washington has rarely seen. According to Sen. Bernie Sanders, coal and oil alone poured $300 million into efforts to kill Build Back Better.

Democrats have another label for Manchin—"corporate democrat." The epithet is well deserved.

Manchin is the 2018 Senate class's top recipient of contributions from lobbyists. He received $512,000 this year, nearly three times as much as last year. He runs again in 2024.

Between 2011 and 2020, the Grinch made about $5 million from his coal-related enterprises, according to an analysis by Open Secrets. Manchin also benefited from a flood of political contributions from the energy industry. He took in more than $400,000 during the July-to-September (2021) fundraising quarter, according to CNN.

As if further evidence is needed, Exxon lobbyists caught on tape... specifically identified Manchin as "their guy" and said they meet with him several times a week.

For another explanation of the reluctance of many to accept the warming for the threat it is, one need to go no further than the tried-and-true Theory of Cognitive Dissonance (1957) in which sociologist Leon Festinger delineated what now seems to be a fairly simple explanation for why it's so difficult to change people's minds or warn them of potential dangers. We all, he said, use built-in mental defense mechanisms to protect us from information we believe to be threatening or that runs contrary to our existing beliefs.

The tools? Selective Exposure, Selective Perception and Selective Retention. In other words, if we can avoid scary or aversive information, we choose not to expose ourselves to it; if we happen to be exposed to aversive information, we change it to fit our preconceived notions; if we are unable to do either, we simply forget it more rapidly than we forget information that's not scary or with which we agree.

To avoid aversive information about the warming, for example, many conservatives choose to expose themselves primarily to Fox "News"—Trump's primary trumpet for spreading lies and disinformation about the climate crisis.

There is also a clear anti-science bias evident in the U.S. population. Response to the COVID pandemic is a case in point. One year after the easy availability of highly effective vaccines, over 30 percent of Americans remained unvaccinated.

The nature of the warming itself also has contributed to people's seeming inability to accept its existence and to consider its negative long-term impact.

There's a simple and well-worn analogy. I'm sure you've heard of the recipe for boiling a frog. If you toss a frog in a pot of boiling water, it will hop out. But if you put it in a pot of lukewarm water and slowly turn up the heat, it will, we're told, boil before it realizes what's happened.

The warming is like that slowly heated pot of water. It's insidious, slow-moving. It has crept up on us. Every slight change in the planet's temperature becomes the "new normal" and is accepted as such. More drought and shrinking water supplies? The new normal. Increases in ocean levels? The new normal. Increasingly violent weather? The new normal.

We must fight against "new normalism" or we'll suffer the same fate as that frog.

Chapter Three

And Where Are We Going?

"For millions of Americans, climate change is no longer just a chart or a graph. It's the smoke on our tongues from massive wildfires. It's the floodwater invading our homes and record-breaking hurricanes and heat waves."

—Jay Inslee, Governor, Washington State

Some numbers to consider: 3.6, 2.12, 425, 8.2, 37 billion, 30, 5.6 million, 1,400.

No, this is not some mysterious code to be cracked. These are individual statistics that help tell the tale of where we are in terms of the warming and that warn about where we're heading.

3.6—Climate scientists had strongly suggested we need to keep the average global temperature increase under 3.6°F (2.0°C) compared to the 1900 benchmark if we were to dodge some of the worst the warming has to offer. But these same scientists have recently lowered the bar to 2.7°F (1.5°C). Unfortunately, as indicated, there is little or no likelihood we can meet either goal. As of this writing, the best available modeling predicts an average global temperature increase of 2.7°F above the 1900 benchmark by 2037. The worst-case scenario for 2100 is a 9.7°F (6°C) increase.

2.12—Earth's global average surface temperature increase in 2023, the highest on record. Continuing the planet's long-term warming trend, the year's globally averaged temperature was 2.12°F (1.18°C) above the twentieth-century average of 57.0°F (13.9°C). And a dramatic drying trend in 2021 pushed a 22-year drought in the U.S. past previous records and shows no signs of easing. This mega-drought deepened so much recently that it is has become the most severe in at least 1,200 years.

425—This ever-increasing number is the parts per million (ppm) concentration of CO_2 in the atmosphere as of this writing. Exceeding 400 ppm has been thought to be the tipping point—the point at which the warming is baked in, irreversible.

8.2—This is the worst-case scenario presented by NOAA for sea-level rise (SLR) by 2100—8.2 feet. It's a warning as to what might be expected if we don't significantly reduce GHG emissions. However, since very little progress has been made in that direction, it may very well be close to an accurate forecast. Since 1900, the oceans have risen about one foot but are rising at an accelerating pace with a three-foot rise not out of the question by 2050.

37 billion—Despite all the dire warnings, humans dumped about 37 billion tons of CO_2 into the atmosphere—a record—in 2023. The forecast for 2024 is 37.5. Less than 30 percent of the world's energy today is provided by alternative non-fossil fuels—solar, wind, nuclear, hydro, thermal and tidal.

30—The number of named tropical storms in the Atlantic and Gulf of Mexico in 2020, a record. There were so many storms that we ran out of names and had to dip into the Greek alphabet for nine additional. Theta was the season's last storm. Though there were fewer storms in 2021, the loss of life and cost of damages incurred were substantially higher than the previous year.

5.6 million—How many acres would you guess burned in wildfires fires in 2021—the worst year on record? Over five million acres went up in smoke. That's almost the equivalent of the total land mass of New Hampshire.

1,400—There is a huge amount of carbon stored in permafrost in the Arctic and Siberian tundra. The Earth's atmosphere now contains about 850 gigatons of carbon. (A gigaton is one billion tons.) There are an estimated 1,400 gigatons of carbon frozen in the rapidly melting tundra. The irony is that human efforts to reduce our output of GHG are likely to be offset by this warming-induced outgassing.

Most of these numbers provide a snapshot the warming's current impact. Others represent forecasts of where the planet is heading. The descriptive numbers—average global temperature increases, annual CO_2 emissions, number of acres burned, for example—are relatively easy to generate. And since detailed records have been kept for many decades, it's possible in many cases to compare what was with what is.

What's much less easy to conjure are the forecasts—the rapidity of temperature increase, how high it may go and how high the oceans may rise. These are the two most essential factors generating the warming's impact and determining just how bad things will become—and when.

The difficulty is that forecasting the impact of the warming is like shooting at a rapidly moving target. The more climate scientists learn about the phenomenon, the more unanticipated variables come to light. And none of them is good. The melting tundra's contribution to the warming's impact is just one example.

Let's look at the implications of the two primary effects of the warming: rising temperatures and sea level rise (SLR).

Rising Temperatures

According to The National Snow and Ice Data Center, on August 14, 2021 temperatures rose above freezing on the summit of the Greenland ice cap, fueling a rain event that dumped seven billion tons of water into the ocean. There is no previous report of rainfall at this location, which reaches 10,551 feet in elevation. The amount of ice lost in one day was seven times more than the daily average for that time of year.

The Earth is home to a range of climates—from the scorching dunes of the Sahara to the glaciers of Greenland. Given this diversity, why are climate scientists alarmed about reaching a worldwide average temperature increase of just 2.7°F (1.5°C) within the next two decades?

Changes in the average temperature of an entire planet, even if just by a few degrees, are significant, according to Peter deMenocal, president and director, Woods Hole Oceanographic Institute.

Earth's climate changes over time. During its 4.6-billion-year lifetime—based on orbital variations, a wobbly axis and other factors—the planet has been a dry world, a water world, an ice world and a fiery Hell. More recently, the last ice age is evidence of its climate variability.

But it's the recent rapid rate of change and the amount of GHG filling the atmosphere that has scientists concerned—concerned enough to recommend that the world should be working to limit the global temperature increase to 2.7°F (1.5°C), a stricter limit than the former goal set by the 2015 Paris agreement.

Overall, Earth was about 2.12°F (1.18°C) warmer in 2023 than in the late nineteenth-century (1850-1900) preindustrial average. A NASA analysis generally matches independent analyses prepared by NOAA and other research groups.

"The Earth is anticipated to exceed the 2.7°F (1.5°C) milestone in about 15 years—between 2032 and 2039. Even over the last 8,000 years, we haven't seen a temperature extreme this rapid and this fast and large," deMenocal said.

As indicated, the worst-case scenario for 2100 is an increase of 9.7°F (6°C) above the baseline.

The first thing to remember is that these are average increases. The reality is that the farther south one goes in the Northern Hemisphere or north in the Southern Hemisphere, the higher the temperatures will range above the average.

The Tropic of Cancer is a line of latitude circling the Earth at approximately 23.5° north of the equator. It is the northernmost point on Earth where the sun's rays can appear directly overhead at local noon. Its southern counterpart is the Tropic of Capricorn. It's the 5,000-plus mile band between these latitudes that will suffer most from increasing temperatures.

Fortunately, the Tropic of Cancer does not touch the U.S. It passes near, but not through, the Hawaiian Islands. But Miami is just 2° north. The fact remains, however, that, as temperatures rise, Miami and Phoenix will be substantially hotter than Seattle and Minneapolis.

One result of these ever-increasing temperatures, of course, has been more drought and desertification in the U.S. and around the planet. Recent U.S. droughts have been the most expansive in decades. At the peak of the 2012 drought—the most extensive since the 1930s—an astounding 81 percent of the contiguous United States was ranked as under at least abnormally dry conditions.

California has experienced a particularly drawn-out drought. Nationwide, conditions reached their peak in December 2020, with the greatest extent of land since 2012 under extreme drought conditions—a drought worsened by heat waves in more than a dozen Western and Central states.

In the West, drought continued and intensified in 2021 exacerbated in the Pacific Northwest by record heat. The drought and heat combined to wither vegetation, aiding the Western wildfires that burned record acreage.

On the world stage, the climate crisis is reducing consumable food calories by around one percent yearly for the top 10 global crops, according to a 2019 study conducted by the University of Minnesota's Institute on the Environment.

"This may sound small, but it represents some 35 trillion calories each year. That's enough to provide more than 50 million people with a daily diet of over 1,800 calories—the level that the UN identifies as essential to avoid food deprivation or undernourishment."

These climatic changes will also drive-up prices. A 2021 study by the Global Sustainability Institute found that, by 2040, food prices will be four times higher than they were in 2000. They're already twice as high as they were then.

The UN has warned that each decade of warming decreases the amount of food the world can produce by two percent, or 4.4 million tons. "Humanity is risking a breakdown of food systems linked to warming—drought, flooding, precipitation variability and extremes."

Sea-level Rise (SLR)

The United States is blessed—some might say cursed—with 13,380 miles of coastline including, of course, the Atlantic, Pacific and Gulf of Mexico. The U.S. ranks eighth in the world in length of coastline.

An estimated 127 million Americans live in coastal counties—almost 40 percent of the population. That's as much as the entire population of Japan. If they were their own nation, the coastal counties of the U.S. would rank third in the world in gross domestic product, beaten only by China and the U.S. as a whole.

This huge U.S. marine economy is fueled by tourism and recreation, offshore energy, shipbuilding, shipping and aquaculture, to name just a few. Many of the country's largest cities are located on these coasts.

It's interesting to note that approximately the same percentage of coastal habitation applies worldwide. It's estimated that 40 percent of the world's population lives within 60 miles of ocean coastline.

The coastal counties in which four in 10 Americans live account for less than 10 percent of the total land mass of the contiguous United States. Coastal areas are far more crowded than the U.S. as a whole; the population density is over five times greater in shoreline counties. Thus warming-related issues that affect the coasts will affect an outsized proportion of Americans.

Obviously, coastal residents face different issues than those living in inland communities. These include SLR induced flooding and hurricanes.

Global SLR began around the start of last century—at about

the same time that warming-induced atmospheric temperature began its inexorable increase. From 1900-2024, the sea level has, on average, risen by about one foot and is accelerating, mostly because the warming is driving thermal expansion of seawater and the melting of land-based ice sheets and glaciers.

According to NOAA, from the 1970s through the last decade or so, melting and heat expansion of water contributed roughly equally to SLR. But the melting of ice sheets has accelerated:

- The average loss of ice from glaciers around the planet quintupled over the past few decades, 6.7 inches of liquid water to 33 inches from 2010-2018.

- Ice loss from the Greenland Ice Sheet increased seven-fold from an average of 34 billion tons per year from 1992-2001 to 247 billion tons per year, 2012-2016.

- Antarctic ice loss nearly quadrupled from an average of 51 billion tons per year from 1992-2001 to 199 billion tons per year, 2012-2016. Scientists worry most about Antarctica because it's nearly twice the size of the United States and contains 90 percent of the earth's ice.

Note that melting Arctic ice is not a factor since it floats—just as melting ice cubes in a glass of water cause no level increase.

It is also important to understand that SLR is not consistent around the planet. For example, generally speaking, levels are rising faster on the U.S. East and Gulf Coasts compared with the West Coast, partially because land along those seaboards is gradually sinking.

The State Most at Risk

Of all locations in the U.S., Florida is the "poster child" for flooding present and future. The state's average height above sea level is only six feet with many areas at or under three feet. Much of the peninsula is slowly sinking, resting as it does primarily on porous limestone.

This has led Climate Central, an independent organization of climate researchers and journalists, to suggest that "the future is now for sea level rise" in Florida.

Based on the accelerating pace of SLR, there are well-considered predictions that *Florida's topography will change from that of a peninsula to an archipelago by 2050* as rising waters fill in lowlands, creating islands.

Florida's state government is aware of the impending crisis but has preferred that it be downplayed. Officials with the Florida Department of Environmental Protection (DEP), the agency responsible for setting its conservation policies and enforcing environmental laws, issued directives several years ago barring its thousands of employees from using the phrases "climate change" and "global warming."

"We were instructed… that we were no longer allowed to use the terms 'global warming' or 'climate change' or even 'sea-level rise'," said a former DEP employee…. "Sea-level rise was to be referred to as 'nuisance flooding'."

According to employee accounts, the ban left damaging information gaps in everything from educational material published by the agency to training programs to annual reports on the environment that could be used to set energy and business policy.

Central to the gag order, of course, was concern about the impact of flooding on real estate values and tourism. Climate Central paints a grim picture of South Florida's economic future, estimating that $5.7 billion in residential property value is at risk of being flooded by 2050 in just Miami Beach alone. Across all of Miami-Dade County, it's closer to $8.7 billion.

Miami-Dade County contains 26 percent of all U.S. homes at risk from rising seas, according to Zillow, an online real estate company.

Worldwide, based on data available in 2017, NOAA predicts a worst-case SLR of approximately three feet by 2050, sufficient to inundate not only Miami but most major coastal cities on the planet. NOAA's nightmare scenario for 2100—over eight feet.

And, as if SLR isn't enough, hurricanes—called cyclones or typhoons in other parts of the world—pose another nightmare.

"Astounding" ocean temperatures in 2023 supercharged "freak" weather around the world as the climate crisis continued to intensify, data reported by *The Guardian* has revealed.

"The oceans absorb 90 percent of the heat trapped by carbon emissions…making it the clearest indicator of global heating. Record levels of heat were taken up by the oceans in 2023, and the data showed that for the past decade the oceans have been hotter every year than the year before.

One result of high ocean water temperatures is the development of hurricanes. It's generally agreed that a surface water temperature of 80°F (27°C) is sufficient to spawn a hurricane. Water off Key West last summer was close to 97°F (36°C).

And early 2024 data was "off the charts."

Worldwide, the U.S. is fifth on the list of countries most affected by these most powerful and damaging of weather events. In a typical year, the U.S. has 12 named storms, six of them hurricanes. Three of these are ranked as major.

But, since all 26 of the letters in the alphabet meteorologists use to name storms were exhausted in 2020, meteorologists began using the Greek alphabet. There were 30, a record.

The 2020 season shattered records across the meteorological board, but one record it didn't break was the cost of damages. At $60-65 billion, it was the fifth costliest season in the past 30 years. The number one season belongs to 2017, which, according to NOAA, caused an estimated $278 billion worth in damages.

These figures, however, are misleading since they include only losses that were greater than insured losses (i.e., not covered by insurance). Widely reported damages caused by Ida in 2021, for example, were $60-65 billion. But catastrophe risk modeler RMS estimates that insured losses from Ida could reach $40 billion, making its true cost closer to $100 billion.

Thus, Ida's damages alone push 2021 ahead of all costs associated with the 2020 season.

A trickle-down effect from a higher number of weather-related claims is insurance rate increases. The State of Louisiana, for example, saw a 23-percent increase in homeowners' insurance premiums after Hurricane Katrina, according to the International Risk Management Institute.

Overall, the cost of homeowners insurance has already increased nearly 50 percent over the past decade. At this rate, the increasing cost of insurance may put it out of reach for many Americans or dramatically increase deductibles they must pay in case of loss.

In any case, many of the losses we are to suffer at the hands of the warming are not insurable.

Section Two will deal with the warming's impact on lifestyle, housing, economics, family finances, food, water, energy, employment, health, safety and security and the coming need for millions of Americans to migrate.

Section Two
Survival of the Fittest

Survival of the Fittest—The continued existence of organisms that are best adapted to their environment, with the extinction of others, as a concept in the Darwinian theory of evolution.

Someone not familiar with Darwin's theory might take "fittest" to mean that only the best physical specimens of a species survive.

That, however, isn't always the case. Individuals that survive aren't necessarily the strongest, fastest or smartest. Darwin didn't mean it in those terms. He intended "fittest" to include members of a species best "adapted" to their immediate environments.

In the context of the warming, those who best survive the warming's civilization-changing impact will be those who have successfully adapted to a changed and changing world. As indicated, to be fit one need not be the strongest, fastest or smartest—although, as will be discussed, being among the very wealthy would be helpful.

The fit will survive the warming by making the adjustments—adaptations—necessary to navigate the dystopian world we see unfolding before our eyes. These adaptations, of course, will not be at the genetic level. "Fit" in this case does not refer to adaptation in the evolutionary sense. Instead, it suggests the need to make those changes in behavior required to adjust to new physical, social, political and economic realities imposed by the warming.

It is the irony of ironies that climate appears to have been the making of humans and now, some two million years later, it may be our undoing!

Most anthropologists believe climate to be a driver of evolutionary change. Since the end of the Miocene there have been only two major "leaps forward" in human evolution—the restructuring of the pelvis and foot allowing our ancestors to have hands free for other things. The second was the rapid expansion of the brain.

Both "leaps" coincided with sudden global shifts towards a colder and drier climate between 3.5 and 2.6 million years ago. In Africa the results were catastrophic. The woodlands were swept away and replaced by an open steppe: a wilderness of sand, patchy grass and thorn bushes.

Thus, it was a change in the climate that brought us down from the trees, requiring that we stand upright and develop the tools and weapons we needed to survive. Will we survive the climate crisis we have created?

Chapter One
"Tis a Gift to be Simple…"

"Tis a Gift to be Simple;
'Tis a Gift to be Free…."
—Shaker Folk Song

The coming decades will require people to make many choices to help them confront challenges the warming is and will present. One of these will certainly be how we chose to live.

There is going to be the pressing need to readjust our expectations— our lifestyles— in order to cope with growing limitations imposed by the warming. There will be the need for people to accept—even embrace— simplicity, self-reliance, sustainability in how we organize our lives to survive in what will be a very different world. This will need to be a multi-generational effort.

A Chicken in Every Pot….

Only once in the history of Presidential elections did a candidate's campaign slogan actually emanate from the opposing party. Such was the fate of the hapless Herbert Hoover in 1928.

"His" slogan—"A chicken in Every Pot and Two Cars in Every Garage"—was not his own. It came from Hoover's bombastic opponent—Al Smith. The Democrats hung it on him based on an unauthorized ad run on his behalf by a local Republican committee—repeating a similar statement that Hoover never actually made. The Democrats sought to embarrass him. But much to the Smith's chagrin, Hoover embraced the slogan and won handily.

More's the pity.

Less than a year into his term, Wall Street came crashing down signaling the beginning of the Great Depression. The crash was caused by excessive speculation and a worldwide economic slowdown in the Roaring Twenties.

Hoover, a dyed-in-wool economic Neanderthal, refused to involve the federal government in fixing prices, controlling banks and businesses, or manipulating the value of the currency—steps that had to wait until 1932 and Franklin Roosevelt whose campaign theme, "Happy Days Are Here Again," helped vault him into the White House. Oddly enough, the song was written in 1929 as a last gasp of optimism before the bottom fell out.

What does any of this have to do with the warming? As Rachel Maddow is wont to say: "Watch this space."

The Roaring Twenties were an exuberant reaction to the gloom and doom imposed on the nation's psyche by World War I and attendant economic travails. Despite the passage of the 18th Amendment with its imposition of Prohibition—1920 through 1933—almost everyone seemed to be having a good time.

Expectations were high and three Republican administrations—Warren Harding, Calvin College and Herbert Hoover—were in no mood to rein in big business.

The bubble burst with the devastating stock market crash on Black Monday, October 28, 1929, when the Dow Jones Industrial Average declined nearly 13 percent. On the following day, Black Tuesday, the market dropped nearly 12 percent. By mid-November, the Dow had lost almost half of its value. The slide continued through the summer of 1932, when the Dow closed at 41.22, its lowest value of the twentieth century, 89 percent below its peak.

And, as if that weren't bad enough, The Dust Bowl period, also known as "the Dirty Thirties," started in 1930 and lasted for about a decade. Its long-term economic impact lingered much longer. Severe drought decimated the Midwest and Southern Great Plains. The massive, choking dust storms began in 1931.

Some thought the advent of a two-theater world war in 1941 would be a blow to the nation's recovery from both the Depression and the Dust Bowl, but World War II had a profound and multifaceted impact on the American economy. It actually lifted the nation out of The Great Depression. As late as 1940, unemployment stood at 14.6 percent; by 1944 it was down to a remarkable 1.2 percent, and the gross national product (GNP) had more than doubled.

Soldiers returned to their jobs or took advantage of the GI Bill to give college a try. Meanwhile, many Rosie the Riveters stayed employed—having learned their career options weren't limited to homemaking, nursing or teaching.

Soon suburbs were sprouting three-bedroom single-family ramblers. While few garages were yet to house two cars, chickens for every pot were plentiful. Expectations were on the rise, including the belief that the new generation of baby boomers would achieve higher levels of success than their parents.

Of course, blips were to come: The Cold War with school children diving under desks to practice hiding from nuclear vaporization; the schismatic Vietnam War; Nixon's Watergate; gas shortages; high inflation in the early '80s; the dot.com meltdown in the late '90s; 9/11; an unjust and costly war in Iraq; a major recession (some say depression) in 2008; the hopelessly inept initial handling of a global pandemic….

But, through it all, optimism has held sway.

Until recently.

It has become apparent that newer generations, generally, will not be as successful as their parents—the Millennials (born 1981-1996) and Generation Z (born 1997-2012), for example. The reasons are varied but include high college debt, limited job opportunities and substantially lower net worth—all resulting for many in continued reliance on parents.

Another significant factor—ever increasing wealth inequality.

It's well known that members of the middle class in America today are worse off than their parents. According to Spendmenot.com: "We looked at the U.S. income inequality statistics and it's clear that the gap of wealth is widening at the expense of the middle class. Since 1970, there have been significant shifts in the balance of wealth:

- The top one percent of earners make 20 times more than the bottom 90 percent.
- The top one percent owns more wealth than the bottom 90 percent combined.
- The top one percent has siphoned away $50 trillion from the bottom 90 percent since 1975."

And optimism about American's future prospects is about to take another hit—the impact on financial resources, both personal and national, resulting from the ever-increasing economic disruption caused by the warming.

Abraham Maslow's Hierarchy of Needs (1943) is a motivational theory in psychology comprising a five-tier model of human needs, often depicted as levels within a pyramid.

From the bottom of the hierarchy upwards, the needs are: *physiological* (food, water, clothing, shelter); *safety* (physical and financial security); *love and belonging* (family, friendship, affiliation); *esteem* (self-worth, respect, accomplishment); and *self-actualization* (realization of potential, self-fulfillment, seeking personal growth and peak experiences).

Needs lower down in the hierarchy must be satisfied to some degree before individuals can ascend to needs higher up. Maslow made it clear that one level of need does not have to be 100 percent realized before a person can begin to "work" on the next.

But Maslow's focus on *needs* failed to consider the fact that much of human behavior is motivated by *wants*. The distinction can easily be made even at the lowest level of the hierarchy. To survive, one needs food, water, clothing and shelter. But do we want to eat roots and berries, dress in animal skins and live in a cave? We all want lifestyles better than that enjoyed by our ancestors 100,000 years ago just as, particularly in economically well-developed countries, younger generations often want—even expect—to enjoy lifestyles superior to that of their parents.

Here's a summary of essential differences between the two motivations:

- Needs are an individual's basic requirements that must be fulfilled in order to survive. Wants are the goods and services an individual would like to have to live well or for status reasons.

- Individuals' needs are limited while their wants are unlimited.

- Needs represent necessities while wants are desires.

- Needs are required for life and do not change with time. Wants are desired either now or in the future. Wants often change and expand over time.

- Wants are not as important as needs because a person can live without satisfying wants.

- Needs are essential for life, so non-fulfillment may lead to illness or death. In contrast, wants are not essential for living, so non-fulfillment does not have as a great an impact.

- However, failure to achieve a want (or wants) often results in disappointment, even depression.

The Gospel According to Mick

Rocker Mick Jagger, in uncharacteristically philosophical lyrics, told fans that sometimes getting what you need is a good substitute for getting what you want. Unfortunately, that could become a motto for the coming world of the warming.

Much of human progress—and that of individuals—has been motivated by the struggle to satisfy wants. It's a thesis of this book that the warming will, over time, require people radically to redefine their expectations.

Fulfilling primary needs such as food, water, clothing and housing will require much more attention than they are now given by most of us. The need to consider the safety of ourselves, our families and others will become more paramount—not just financial security but physical safety from the warming's climatic onslaught and the increased violence that is bound to ensue.

Thus, as indicated, there will be the need to redefine expectations and embrace simplicity, self-reliance, sustainability as means to survive in what will be a very different world.

One of the most popular categories of books found on "Self Help" shelves at bookstores or through online booksellers preaches the doctrine of simplification. And I'm not talking about books proposing that one simplify by buying and installing—or having installed—elaborate shelving systems to help organize all your stuff.

Many hold the belief that modern life is crazy—particularly in the so-called developed world. For the record, here are a few facts about the anxiety drug Xanax:

- Doctors write 50 million prescriptions a year for the family of drugs to which Xanax belongs.

- Xanax is the fifth most prescribed drug in the U.S.

- Over 125,000 people visit U.S. emergency rooms every year because of complications related to their Xanax use. The number of annual hospital admissions that are directly related to Xanax use—60,000.

- Prescription rates for Xanax have been climbing at a nine percent annual rate since 2008.

Anxiety, depression and other mental disorders run rampant throughout our society. A primary reason? Many are overwhelmed by the rapid-paced, super-complex and stuff-filled lives they've created for themselves. Instead, the warming will require that we build lifestyles appropriately scaled to increasing scarcity—lives that are self-sustaining and realistic based on the reduction in options the warming will bring. We will need to become more self-reliant and be able to do for ourselves that which we have relied on others to do.

Don't worry. I'm not going to preach against the evils of materialism and consumerism. Wanting things—and ever more things—is a basic human trait. Given the resources, people will tend to extend their list of "wants" for reasons of increasing comfort, convenience, aesthetics, status. The point here is that the warming will increasingly limit access to wants and redirect peoples' efforts toward satisfying basic needs.

A Family Warming Coach?

If a family or extended family wishes to undertake the mission of preparing to weather the disruptions the warming will bring, some family member needs to take the lead and, for lack of better title, become the family "warming coach"—the individual responsible for the development of a plan with the input of others and in overseeing its implementation.

That, of course, sounds simpler than it is. First, in modern-day America, most families are spread out geographically, requiring, in many cases, Zoom or similar online meetings. And there is another reality that must be faced. Families rarely follow the "Father Knows Best," or "Leave it to Beaver" sitcom model of the typical 1950s family. Many families are dysfunctional to some extent, making the job of organizing an approach to the warming more difficult. It is possible, of course, that fighting the warming may bring families closer together in a common cause.

In any case, the family must be convinced that something needs to be done. Then comes planning and implementation that may take several generations, with modifications along the way. So, the job of warming coach will need to be handed down from generation to generation—a passing of the baton. (See the Discussion Guide, Appendix A)

Let's consider just one of many possible lifestyle changes.

If I write "commune" (and, of course, I just did), what immediately comes to mind? If you said "hippies" you'd join the majority of the folks to whom I've posed the question.

Other responses are also interesting: "sex, drugs, rock 'n roll;" "turn on, tune In and drop out," "flower children," "wilted daisies stuck in the working ends of M-16s," "a rainy Woodstock with wet t-shirts or no t-shirts," "psychedelic VW buses" ….

I'm guessing the responses depended a lot on whether respondents experienced hippiedom firsthand, had watched it unfold from the sidelines or, much later, in numerous documentaries.

But, generally, the attitude toward communes—as a manifestation of hippie culture—is not a positive one. Most came and went quickly. Most failed because they were unable to facilitate—in a practical way—the freedom from convention their inhabitants sought; the escape from the grinding, disheartening realities of 1960s life.

Then, of course, "dropouts" make lousy leaders—something successful communes need.

In following years, the reputation of communes was further besmirched. Do the names Jim Jones, David Koresh or Warren Jeffs ring any bells? I won't spend much time on these esteemed gentlemen, except to point out that the concept of the "commune" suffered greatly at their hands.

A Commune Hall of Shame

The Jonestown Massacre occurred in November, 1978, when more than 900 members of an American cult called the Peoples Temple died in a mass suicide-murder under the direction of their leader *Jim Jones*. It took place at the so-called Jonestown settlement in the South American nation of Guyana.

In April, 1993, some 75 members of the millennial sect known as the Branch Davidians—including their messianic leader, *David Koresh*—perished in a blaze that destroyed their compound near Waco, Texas, after a 51-day siege by federal agents. He had become the subject of allegations of polygamy and child sexual abuse at the commune, although investigators found no conclusive evidence.

Warren Jeffs is the infamous president and "prophet" of the Fundamentalist Church of Jesus Christ of Latter-Day Saints, an offshoot of the Mormon Church, notorious for polygamy and child brides. In addition to its Texas commune—the "Yearning for Zion" ranch—sects were also based in Utah and Arizona. In 2008, FBI and Texas authorities raided the compound, gathering enough evidence to convict him on sexual assault charges. In 2011, the prophet was sentenced to life plus 20 years in prison.

The reality, however, is that the term "commune" has almost always had negative connotations—even as far back as the founding in 1825 of New Harmony in Indiana by British industrialist Robert Owen to test his theories of socialism. The commune suffered under his high-handed leadership, dissention about governance and the role religion should play. It also apparently suffered from the laziness of many residents who preferred to enjoy the beauties of nature to getting food on the table. It lasted about three years, but, eventually, morphed into today's town of New Harmony.

American's attitudes toward communes or communal living are interesting, considering the fact that humans have always been communal livers. In hunter-gatherer days—after we'd stopped dragging our knuckles and stood up on our own two feet—we lived together in small bands much as our Chimpanzee ancestors had done for many millennia.

In fact, a case could be made that communal living is what saved humans from extinction.

Pity our poor forbears. Almost naked they stood—small, weak, not particularly fleet of foot, essentially weaponless—against some of the most efficient predators on the African savannah, particularly the big cats.

Fossils indicate these saber-toothed nightmares dined regularly on our ancestors. Several skulls have been unearthed showing two precisely spaced holes that perfectly match the long incisors of *Dinofelis*, a cat slightly smaller than a lion that may have specialized in hunting humanoids.

It would be thousands of years before our newly enlarged brains and dexterous hands could fashion weapons needed to equalize the odds; to catch up in the arms race. Until then, early humans had to stick together.

According to Ib'n Khakdūn: "Whereas God gave animals their natural limbs for defence, he gave man the ability to think. The power of thought allowed him to manufacture weapons…and to organize communities for producing them. Since any one individual was powerless against the…predatory animal, man could only protect himself through communal defence."

The same strategy that may have saved our species two million years ago may need to be employed again, this time to save many of us from folly we have brought down on our own heads—the warming.

It's not difficult to predict that communes, communal living, or as modern jargon would have it— "intentional communities"— will be a significant survival tactic as the evils of the warming are visited upon us.

Perhaps because of its negative connotations, the Foundation for Intentional Community (FIC) has chosen to call communes "intentional communities." The FIC defines an intentional community as a group of people who have chosen to live together or share resources on the basis of common values.

"Intentional communities model more cooperative, sustainable and just ways of life."

For two decades, the foundation has been a major resource internationally for communal organizations—either already formed or forming. Its website provides details for over 200 of its some 1,000 intentional community members.

Categories include:

- **Ecovillages**–Generally communities with a strong ecological focus.

- **Cohousing**–Communities that incorporate both private homes and shared common facilities, supporting neighborly connections.

- **Communes**–The FIC hasn't discarded the "commune" designation but restricts it to communities that are 100 percent income sharing.

- **Co-ops**–Communities that are cooperative, generally expense sharing, often urban with shared housing. Many focus on college students.

- **Religious**–Communities that identify as spiritual or religious in nature. Jewish and Christian communities are most common.

As I hope succeeding chapters demonstrate, the financial impact of the warming, its negative effects on our social, political and physical infrastructures, its disruption of what we have come to expect as our way of life and our expectations for future generations, will make plain the advantages of coming together in forms of communities that enable sharing of resources and skill sets for the good of community members.

The benefits are obvious and revolve primarily around cost savings. A lot, of course, depends on the size of a community and how it's structured, but the following are examples of benefits of communal living:

- Communities can be as self-sustaining as their inhabitants choose to make them through, for example, communal agriculture.
- Going entirely off-grid—or as much as possible—removes or reduces what will certainly be the increasing undependability and higher costs of utilities.
- Communities can develop business or manufacturing enterprises that provide income or bartering opportunities for financial support.
- Depending on the financial structure that's established, a variety of expenses can be shared.
- A community's children can be home-schooled by qualified residents.
- Basic health care can be provided if the community includes a resident health care professional. Depending on the size of the community, inexpensive group health insurance may be obtained.
- In numbers there can be increased safety and security. There's no need to tell you that America is already a violent place. But, unfortunately, as the warming fires up, there will be increasing violence—particularly directed at those who have by those who have not. At some point, providing security for residents will become a primary function of a community.

Taking advantage of intentional communities will not be easy. Communes, or whatever you choose to call them, do not have a great track record of long-term success. In fact, there are estimates that only 10 percent last more than 10 years. And pointing to success factors is made difficult by the great variety of organizational structures and variabilities between the communities.

A few of the more obvious:

- **Effective, consensual leadership.** Managing any human organization can be a nightmare and an intentional community is no exception. Depending on the size and relative complexity of the community, managers can be elected for limited terms, or a small board of directors could be selected and appoint an executive director from its ranks. Please, no prophets or charismatics.

- **Work, work, work.** All members of the community must share in its labors as equally as possible. Age-appropriate work should be available for the young and old. A mechanism should be available for dealing with limited-contributors—up to and including expulsion.

- **Vet potential new members**—particularly if they are not family or close friends. New members who turn out to be incompatible with the goals of the community or with other members, obviously, are disruptive.

At this point you may not be able to accept communal living as an important tool in the warming-survival toolbox. It is probably difficult to imagine the need at some point for you or your progeny to join forces with others in some manner—whether extended family, friends or strangers—better to survive the dystopian future the warming will bring.

Nor perhaps can you readily accept the need to downgrade expectations and embrace simplicity, self-reliance, sustainability as a means to survive in what will be a very different world. But, I fear, such an adjustment will be necessary.

The following fictional television vignette—one of several in the book—takes a close look the communal lifestyles that have been part of the American landscape since the 1800s. Camera directions are spelled out but may be ignored in favor of just reading the narrative.

Kent Whitaker Reporting
Environmental News Network
August 19, 2047, 5:35 p.m. CDT

NEW HARMONY

Anchor: Senior Editor Kent Whitaker has filed a two-part report from an undisclosed location. He will explain why all the secrecy.

Cut to video

Camera One Medium Shot (MS) of Whitaker standupper

Whitaker: I'm standing here enjoying an old-fashioned summer's day in this bucolic rural setting. I haven't heard cicadas in a long time.

Camera One zooms to Long Shot (LS), slow pan right to follow Whitaker

Whitaker Voice Over (VO): The sweet corn growing beyond this split-rail fence should be ready for harvest in less than a month. As you can see, farmers are at work weeding a large vegetable plot. Farther on, there's a cluster of red outbuildings and, across the fields, white farm homes.

Continue LS pan with Whitaker, interviewee walks into frame, zoom to MS

Whitaker: Joining me is Jack Braden who is a founder of New Harmony. Jack, why have you asked us not to disclose your location?

Braden: I know this will sound elitist, but—as your viewers will see—we have a good thing going here. And there are only so many people who can enjoy it. We hate to be put in a position to have to turn people away. We've already had some of that.

Camera Two cut to Whitaker Close Up (CU)

Whitaker: I suggested earlier that New Harmony is a commune. But you objected to the term. If it's not a commune, what is it?

Camera One cut to Braden CU

Braden: Let's just say the term has negative connotations. Over the years—even as far back as the founding of our namesake in 1825—communes have not worked. One of the first major commune experiments was New Harmony in Indiana. It lasted only about three years.

Camera Two cut to Whitaker CU reaction

Braden (VO): Then—in more recent times—there were the hippie communes of the '60s and '70s. Many were started to reflect the idealism of the time—rejecting materialism, living off the land, taking care of the environment. But the primary rationale for most was freedom from social norms—freedom to do drugs, freedom to be promiscuous, freedom to do their own thing. And, of course, almost all failed in short order.

Camera Two stay on Whitaker CU

Whitaker: Okay, then what are you?

Camera One cut to Braden CU

Braden: We are a community and a company. We are incorporated as New Harmony, Inc. We pay taxes just as does any other company. Our main focus is the agricultural and animal products that we sell in the region. We also sell honey and honey-based products online—when the Internet is up and running.

Camera One slow zoom back to MS

Whitaker: You mentioned the hippie's rationale for communal living was freedom from social norms. What's New Harmony's reason for being?

Braden: In a word—survival. Most of us here were jobless with bleak futures—the result of the warming-induced economic meltdown. For example, I was in real estate. Others had jobs in manufacturing, retail, teaching—all hard hit. Some of our members lost homes to flooding. The initial founders five years ago were friends and friends of friends looking for a way to pool resources to save our families. New Harmony was the answer. So, you can see that our commitment is serious and abiding.

Whitaker: So, how many residents live here and what are the criteria for joining?

Braden: We now number about 125 living in 17 households with our singles in dormitories. As I said earlier, we are about full up. Our land won't support additional housing without endangering the environment and limiting the land we have to cultivate. To your second question, residents had to meet strict admission standards. The amount of money they could put into the communal pot was important, but, frankly, not as important as whether they had needed skills—farming, animal husbandry, cooking, weaving, sewing, construction, teaching, nursing and so on. Everyone also was required to take a battery of psychological tests to be as sure as possible they would fit in.

Whitaker: And how are you governed?

Camera Two cut to Braden CU

Braden: We elect a small board that appoints a chair. All major company and community decisions are made consensually at regular meetings of the resident stockholders.

Camera One cut to Whitaker CU

Whitaker: May I ask how you're doing financially?

Camera Two zoom to MS

Braden: Well, we're finally breaking even. Initially the property was a disaster. The aquifer in the area had dried up and the owner couldn't afford to extend the well deeper for irrigation. He lost the property in foreclosure, and it was vacant for quite some time. Much of the initial investment of the founding families went to deepen the well and install wind and solar power. We lived hand-to-mouth for the first few years. It's taken a lot of very hard work to reach this point, but it's been worth it.

Whitaker: And to what do you attribute your success?

Camera One cut to Braden CU

Braden: Early on we took a careful look at what made communes fail. There seemed to be two primary reasons—ineffective leadership and the laziness of residents. We have solved those problems through election and rotation of company-community leaders, governance by consensus and ensuring that our members work and work very hard. Non-contribution to necessary labor is a reason for expulsion. New Harmony didn't just happen. Everyone puts in 8-10 hours a day, six days a week. Even children have age-appropriate chores.

Camera Two cut to Whitaker CU

Whitaker: Your population is small. Surely you don't have the expertise to cover all your needs.

Camera One zoom to MS

Braden: Absolutely true. At present we lack an automotive mechanic to keep our various trucks and farm equipment running. So, we barter with a local mechanic—food for his services. Same is true of maintaining our solar and wind systems. Barter, as you know, is becoming more and more common as a way of getting what you need if you have no money.

Whitaker: You said earlier that you're now breaking even. If there is profit, where will it go?

Braden: If the consensus is that we plow it back into the community, we will. Or we may take a portion and distribute it equally among the stockholders. **Cut to anchor**

Anchor: I hope you'll watch part two of Kent's visit to New Harmony tomorrow night at 5:45 p.m. CDT. Josh will take Kent on a tour including the farm operation, dining hall, school, honey processing and packing facility, as well as a visit with a recently arrived family.

Cut to commercial

Chapter Two
"Location, Location, Location!"

Within 50 years, extremely hot zones like the Sahara could cover nearly one-fifth of the planet, placing about a third of the world's population outside the climate niche in which we have prospered for thousands of years. This will lead to a migration the likes of which humankind has never seen.

About a billion people around the world live within 60 miles of a coastline and face the threat of inundation as the oceans continue their inexorable rise.

"Location, location, location." Harold Samuel coined this—the most famous of all real estate slogans—in 1944 when he founded Land Securities, one of the United Kingdom's largest property companies.

Location in real estate is important because it's thought that being near good schools, retail, restaurants, recreation and scenic views is important in residential property evaluations. The closer a property is to such places; the more buyers will pay for it.

The warming, however, is adding new meaning to the phrase. Eventually, *location* for billions of Earth's inhabitants will eventually mean *re-location* to areas of the globe not being ravaged—or being ravaged less—by the adverse effects of the climate crisis. In the new real estate scheme of things, *safety* will trump other currently prized factors in helping people decide where they should live.

Humans have been blessed with opposing thumbs and big brains allowing us, among many other things, to create livable environments where we might not have otherwise survived. For most of us, particularly those living in wealthier nations, it's difficult to imagine life without central heating and air conditioning.

But for most of human history people have lived within a surprisingly narrow range of mean average temperatures (52°-58°F / 11°-15°C) in places where the climate supported abundant food production. As the planet warms, however, that comfort zone is narrowing.

According to a recent study in the *Proceedings of the National Academy of Sciences*, the planet could see a greater temperature increase in the next 50 years than it did in the last 6,000 combined. A 2017 study in *Science Advances* warns that by 2100 temperatures could rise to the point that just going outside for a few hours in some places... "will result in death even for the fittest of humans."

People are already beginning to flee. In Southeast Asia, where increasingly unpredictable monsoon rainfall, cyclones and drought have made life more difficult, the World Bank points to more than eight million people who have moved toward the Middle East, Europe and North America. In the African Sahel, millions of rural people have been streaming toward the coasts and the cities amid drought and widespread crop failures.

Should the flight away from hot climates reach the scale that current research suggests, it will amount to a vast remapping of the world's population.

Meanwhile, in the U.S., many people seem to be migrating in the *wrong direction*. For years Americans have avoided confronting climatic changes in their own backyards. The decisions we make about where to live are distorted not just by politics that play down climate risks, but also by the availability of flood and fire insurance, technology and other incentives aimed at defying nature.

In much of the developing world, in contrast, vulnerable people are attempting to flee the emerging perils of the warming, seeking cooler temperatures, more fresh water and safety. But in the U.S., many people continue to gravitate *toward* environmental danger, building, for example, along coastlines and settling in the cloudless deserts of the Southwest.

There will be a price. Migration for many Americans is inevitable.

Probably the most important decision you or members of your family will make in terms of how well you and your future generations deal with the warming is where you choose to live.

We live where we live for a wide variety of reasons. Perhaps our jobs have taken us there. Or we may have a strong emotional or historical attachment to the area. Or our "people" are there. Perhaps it's a fondness for the geography—be it ocean, lake, river, mountain or wide-open spaces. Or the climate. Or maybe you're simply stuck because you can't afford to move. Any of these or others may be factors.

As indicated earlier, *safety* for most of us is probably not now a consideration in making real estate decisions—unless, of course, you happen to live in an urban area plagued by an increasingly high-crime rate. If, however, you were paying attention to the negative effects of the warming detailed earlier, I hope you've come to realize that the safety of where you and yours live should become of paramount concern.

Unless you've had first-hand experience with warming-related catastrophes—hurricanes, floods, tornados, drought, wildfires and the like—you may not be inclined to think about the need to relocate, even if it's at some point in the future. Or you may be fortunate enough to live in what may be a relatively safe area, minimizing the need to consider eventual relocation.

I happen to live in one of the areas that could be deemed safer than most—Minnesota. Of course, as I write this, the temperature is 16°F and we just dug out of a 10-inch snowfall. But, overall, Minnesota is a better bet for beating the warming than Florida.

Age is also a factor. You may be of an age—like mine—that makes relocation less urgent. I am well into my senior citizenship and, unless I live into my hundreds, I should have shed this mortal coil before the worst of the warming is underway. That doesn't mean, however, that those in their "golden years" shouldn't be having frank discussions with offspring about where—considering the warming— they should choose to hang their hats.

"Sooner" Better Than Later

"Sooners" was the name given to settlers who entered unassigned lands in what is now the State of Oklahoma before the official start of the Land Rush of 1889. These lands were part of Native American territory that, after a lobbying campaign, were opened to settlement by land-hungry white settlers.

The designation "sooner" initially had negative connotations because these cheaters snuck out early and stole better land from other settlers. However, by the time of statehood, "sooner" had become an affectionate term for Oklahomans. In 1908, the University of Oklahoma football team adopted the nickname "Sooners" and the state has come to be known as the "Sooner" state.

The coming migrations of Americans fleeing the negative effects of the climate crisis will not resemble the land rush of 1889. This massive relocation will take place over decades as conditions worsen. But, clearly, in order to acquire the best and safest new living arrangements, sooner will be better than later.

According to research by the *New York Times* and *ProPublica*: "Across the United States, some 162 million people—nearly 1 in 2—will most likely experience a decline in the quality of their environment, namely more heat and less water. For 93 million of them, the changes could be particularly severe, and by 2070, our analysis suggests...at least four million Americans could find themselves living at the fringe, in places decidedly outside the ideal niche for human life."

What, specifically, are the implications for the U.S. of a global mean temperature increase by 2037 of almost 3°F (1.6°C) above the 1900 norm? What about almost 10°F (5.1°C) by 2100?

The effects of temperature increase are already plain for all to see. In the U.S. they include decades of deep and deepening drought, annual wildfire epidemics, loss of biodiversity and, as discussed, the nightmare posed by SLR—flooding and the increasing number and severity of hurricanes.

Unseasonably warm temperatures when mixed with a frigid sagging jet stream—an increasingly common weather pattern—also result in weather mayhem.

The tornadoes that ripped across the central and southern U.S. late in the evening of December 10, 2021, were notable in many ways. These thunderstorms and tornadoes traveled far—sometimes more than 100 miles—and the effects were widespread. NOAA confirmed that the massive storm front produced 61 tornadoes. The very fact that tornadoes of this intensity struck in late autumn, rather than in the spring and summer when they are most likely, is remarkable.

Eight states—Kentucky, Arkansas, Tennessee, Missouri, Illinois, Georgia, Ohio and Indiana— reported tornadoes that killed more than 80 people and brought devastating damage to many communities.

These were very strong winds and storms because a powerful disturbance in the jet stream created an intense low-pressure system. But low pressure wasn't what made this event unusual. It was unprecedented because vast amounts of warm air got pulled up from the Gulf of Mexico and collided with the sagging jet stream to create a storm front hundreds of miles long.

Another temperature-driven problem is drought. Dry conditions are a natural part of the climate cycle, but as Earth's atmosphere continues to warm, droughts are becoming more frequent, severe and pervasive. The past 20 years, for example, have seen some of the driest conditions in the American West on record and that will likely have long-term impact on the land and the people who depend on it.

Heat Apocalypse

In July, 2022 hundreds of millions of people around the world sweltered in extreme heat as record-breaking heat waves set swathes of Europe's countryside on fire, scorched the U.S. and put dozens of Chinese cities under alert.

The Europeans dubbed the event the "heat apocalypse" as the brutal heat wave brought record-breaking temperatures to parts of France, Portugal, the United Kingdom and Spain and more than 1,000 heat-related deaths. Several wildfires also burned thousands of acres, including two massive blazes in southwestern France fueled by dry pines and erratic winds.

Five separate high-pressure weather systems across the northern hemisphere, which were linked by atmospheric waves, led to unprecedented temperatures on multiple continents. The UK smashed its all-time heat mark (104.5°F / 62.5°C), as did several cities in Texas and Oklahoma. Wichita Falls reached a broiling 115°F (69°C).

The heat waves have led some to ask if the warming is heating up faster than expected. This prompted MIT in its *Technology Review* to maintain that "the recent heat waves were a stress test for the modeling of extreme events."

As noted earlier, about 127 million Americans—almost 40 percent of the population—live in ocean-side counties encompassing only 10 percent of the country's land mass. As the waters rise, it's people in these areas—both urban and rural—who will be most affected.

SLR alone will not be the culprit. Flooding during higher-than-normal tides and storm surges driven by tropical storms and hurricanes will do much of the damage. Heavy rainfall well inland also contributes to flood damage.

Hurricane Katrina in 2005 created one of the most devastating storm surges in U.S. history. It peaked at 28 feet, scouring the Mississippi town of Pass Christian off the face of the planet. Some 90 percent of all structures were flattened or damaged beyond repair. The surge was so powerful it lifted off slabs covering graves in a Civil War-era cemetery and literally sucked the coffins out. The massive wave penetrated six miles inland across much of southern Mississippi and up to 12 miles along bays and rivers.

This is the same storm that killed 1,500 in Louisiana and put 70 percent of New Orleans underwater. The city is an average of six feet below sea level and slowly sinking. Total damage estimates for Katrina—$125 billion.

After Katrina, the federal government spent $14.5 billion on projects designed to enhance protection from storm surge and flooding in New Orleans and surrounding suburbs. Thus far the improved protection has helped the city and environs withstand subsequent hurricane activity. But, considering the subsidence of the area and continued loss of barrier islands and marshes along the coast, the future is not bright.

The U.S. Atlantic coast is also not immune to destructive hurricanes. Sandy, in 2012, earned the nickname "Frankenstorm" since it wreaked havoc in 24 states on its march from the central Caribbean, across Jamaica, Cuba and the Bahamas and up the Eastern seaboard. The highest storm surge in New York City was measured at the tip of Manhattan—14 feet. The resulting flooding knocked out the subway system and closed all but one tunnel entering Manhattan. The storm killed 285 and caused an estimated $75 billion in damages.

Unfortunately, as demonstrated recently by Hurricane Ida (2021)—the fifth most destructive hurricane to hit the U.S.— increasingly these Frankenstorms do not limit death and destruction to the coastlines where they initially hit.

Instead Ida continued trekking inland from Louisiana, eventually making its way to the Northeast, delivering heavy rainfall that flooded streets, homes and neighborhoods. Local and state officials scrambled to respond to the storm's fierce second punch. At least 52 people died across New York, New Jersey, Connecticut, Maryland, Pennsylvania and Virginia. In contrast, only 11 were killed in Louisiana where it initially hit.

"New York City literally has been paralyzed," New York Gov. Kathy Hochul told CNN. "Unprecedented is almost an understatement. This is the first time ever we've had a flash flood emergency declared."

In 2022, The National Hurricane Center announced that Hurricane Ian attained Category 5 status with 160 mph sustained winds for a few hours before weakening slightly and hitting Florida west coast as a devastating Cat 4.

Total damages from Ian are estimated at $112.9 billion, making it the third-most expensive weather disaster in world history. Only Hurricane Katrina of 2005 ($190 billion) and Hurricane Harvey of 2017 ($151 billion) were more expensive. Ian's deaths totaled 156.

As the hurricane crossed Florida from southwest to northeast, it dumped an enormous amount of rain causing serious flooding in central and eastern Florida where rainfall totals of 10-20 inches caused major river flooding. Daytona Beach recorded rainfall of 21.5 inches.

America's flooding capital, however, would seem to be Houston. Though 40 miles from the Gulf, Houston has a long history of hurricane-related extreme rainfall events—including many in recent years. It's the sixth most populous city in the U.S.

In 2019, tropical storm Imelda had winds no stronger than 45 mph as it made landfall along the upper Texas coast. But it slowed its forward speed to less than five mph the following day and meandered all over east Texas. That slow movement produced over 30 inches of rain in several counties across southeast Texas, including the Houston and Beaumont areas.

Warming-related events like tropical storms and hurricanes are normally associated with warm-weather months. But don't tell that to residents along the U.S. Northeast Coast. Winter storms that emerge off the Atlantic will occasionally strengthen very quickly, bringing strong winds, heavy snow accumulations and flooding. Such intense storms are called "bomb cyclones."

From 1979 to 2019 about seven percent of winter storms that developed in North America were categorized as bomb cyclones. They begin in the temperate latitudes and strengthen fast with the atmospheric pressure at the center dropping swiftly, a process now called "bombogenesis."

The Northeast was pummeled by one of the worst bomb cyclones on record in January, 2022. Winds in some areas reached 80 mph. Snow accumulations broke records in Massachusetts, New Jersey, New York and Pennsylvania. Boston was hit by 24 inches of snow in 24 hours. Hundreds of thousands were without power, roads were impassable, thousands of flights were cancelled as was Amtrak service between New York and Washington.

Chapter Three
Go North, Young Man, Go North

"There is nothing more important than a good, safe, secure home."
—Rosalynn Carter

One of the nicest things about writing for the web versus print is that, on the Internet, one can provide direct links to important resources. Books, obviously, do not offer that capability—except to list links and suggest that readers take them to their browsers.

As of this writing there are many detailed online reports of research suggesting how the warming will affect various U.S. locations. And, of course, many more will come in the months and years to come.

These studies present data about expected temperature increases over time and suggest the impact of those rising temperatures on human comfort, health and productivity. They also forecast the negative impact of higher temperatures on water resources, agriculture, livestock production and wildfire activity.

Other studies predict the inundation of many areas along our more than 13,000 miles of coastline. Still others detail the growing impact of meteorological phenomena such as hurricanes and other forms of severe weather, while others focus on the effect of the warming on our economy and infrastructure.

One of the most comprehensive and visually graphic reports

came from *ProPublica* and the *New York Times* in September, 2020: https://projects.propublica.org/climate-migration/

The online report features interactive maps that illustrate changes for key climate parameters in the U.S. over time. *It also provides readers with the ability to review forecast changes in their own counties.*

Overall, the data—provided by Rhodium Group—warns that rising temperatures and changing rainfall patterns will drive temperate climates and agriculture northward, while SLR will consume coastlines and dangerous levels of humidity will swamp the Mississippi River valley.

"…other recent research show(s) that the most habitable climate in North America will shift northward and the incidence of large fires will increase across the country, (suggesting) that the climate crisis will profoundly interrupt the way we live and farm in the United States."

In the U.S. today, the "human climate niche"—the region where temperature and precipitation have been most suitable for humans for the past 6,000 years—blankets the heart of the country from the Atlantic seaboard through northern Texas and Nebraska and then skips over to California's coastal regions.

But as the climate warms, the report indicates the niche could shift drastically northward. By 2070, under even a moderate carbon emissions scenario, much of the Southeast, Deep South and Southwest would become less suitable as the niche shifts north. In the case of extreme warming, the niche moves more quickly toward Canada, leaving much of the lower half of the U.S. too hot or dry for the type of climate in which humans historically have lived.

Heat is one of the largest drivers changing the niche of human habitability. Researchers estimate that between 2040 and 2060 extreme temperatures will become commonplace in the South and Southwest, with some counties in Arizona experiencing temperatures above 95 degrees for half the year.

The First Heat Czar

"When it comes to extreme heat, Phoenix, AZ, is shattering just about every record. Temperatures last week (June, 2022) exceeded 110°F (66°C) on four days straight, breaking two daily records. Nighttime temperatures never fell below 80°F (48°C). On many days, the sidewalks are hot enough to burn dogs' paws," according to *The Guardian*.

Extreme heat is the leading cause of climate-related deaths in the US. Heat-related deaths in Maricopa County, where Phoenix is located, are up 70 percent from 2019, reaching 662 in the last two years. But unlike floods and hurricanes, extreme heat is not eligible for federal emergency funding.

Today, millions of Arizonans are getting used to record-breaking heat. Just this decade, Phoenix has set new daily heat records on 33 different days, which is significantly more than any previous decade in recorded history.

It's not just for highs, though. The city has set new records for hottest minimum daily temperatures 44 times as well—and that's just since 2010.

In response, Phoenix has appointed a "heat czar"—the first such role in the US – who is tasked with finding ways to make the city more livable in the summer.

But heat alone won't determine Americans' fate.

The *ProPublica* and *New York Times* report presents a new climate analysis that projects how humidity and heat collide to form "wet bulb" temperatures that will disrupt daily existence. When heat meets excessive humidity, the body can no longer cool itself by sweating. High wet bulb temperatures make it dangerous to work and play outdoors. As wet bulb temperatures increase, so does the risk of heat stroke—and even death.

"Today, the combination of truly dangerous heat and humidity is rare. But, by 2050, parts of the Midwest and Louisiana could see conditions that make it difficult for the human body to cool itself for nearly one out of every 20 days in the year."

The report suggests that heat and humidity in Missouri will feel like Louisiana does today, while some areas we don't usually think of as humid—like southwestern Arizona—will see soaring wet bulb temperatures because of factors such as sun angle, wind speed and cloud cover reacting to high temperatures.

New projections for farm productivity also indicate that growing food will become difficult across large parts of the country, including the heart of the High Plains' (also known as the Southern Great Plains) $35 billion agriculture industry. Meanwhile, the northern Midwest and Great Plains may gain short-term benefits in farm productivity and in overall comfort.

Rising temperatures will make it more difficult to grow corn and soy, the most prevalent crops in the U.S. They are the basis for livestock feed and other staple foods, and they have critical economic significance. Because of their broad regional spread, they offer the best proxy for predicting how farming will be affected by rising temperatures and changing water supplies.

Corn and soy production is sensitive to heat and will decrease for every degree of warming. By midcentury, North Dakota, which already harvests millions of acres of both crops, will warm enough to allow for more growing days and higher yields. But parts of Texas and Oklahoma, for example, may see yields drop by more than 70 percent.

"With heat and ever more prevalent drought, the likelihood is that the number of very large wildfires will increase substantially, particularly in the West, Northwest and the Rocky Mountains, but also in Florida, Georgia and the Southeast," according to the report.

All the while, SLR will transform the coasts.

As the ocean rises, the amount of submerged coastline increases dramatically, affecting a small sliver of the nation's land but a disproportionate share of its population. As indicated, an estimated

127 million Americans live in coastal counties—almost 40 percent of the population. Some 50 million live in eight of the largest U.S. metro areas—Miami, New York and Boston among them—all of which lie in some of the most affected counties in the U.S.

"Populous cities with expensive real estate, including Houston and Miami, will see damage tallied in the billions—losses worth several percentage points of GDP—largely driven by storms, sea level rise...," according to the *ProPublica* and *New York Times* report.

"Combined, these factors will lead to profound economic losses—and possibly mass migration of Americans away from distress in much of the southern and coastal regions of the country."

It doesn't take a real estate genius to translate all these quite plausible warming-related warnings into advice about "location, location, location."

Clearly location or relocation decisions should lead Americans away from coastal areas—particularly on the Atlantic and the Gulf. And all indications are that the human "habitable niche" will move north as temperatures increase, making the Southeast, Deep South and Southwest significantly less hospitable. In some areas high temperatures and humidity will combine to make life very uncomfortable—even dangerous.

Meanwhile dryness and drought conditions in other areas will result in water shortages, increase the likelihood of wildfires and disrupt agriculture.

Okay, so where's safe?

At this point, the best one can do is speculate. Considering factors such as proximity to ocean coastlines, potential future temperatures, water availability and the likelihood for extreme weather, the best bets would be the Northwest, northern Rocky Mountain States, northern Upper Midwest, and north and northeast of the Ohio Valley.

As a general rule, Americans put a great deal of faith in technology. We've been accustomed to constant technological progress. There are those, therefore, who expect that science and technology will yet find a way to save us from the worst of the warming. That's a comforting but false hope.

The reality is that we have had the technological answers to arresting the warming at our fingertips for many decades, even more than a century in one case. They are power derived from solar, wind, nuclear, hydroelectric and tidal and thermal energy sources. Sadly, we've chosen not to make sufficient use of them in time.

Weather-related damage and destruction, limited water resources, poor crop yields, lower labor productivity, health issues and increasing crime are among the climate-driven elements that will likely drag down the U.S. economy, eventually taking a financial toll that may exceed personal and governmental financial resources. They are also the factors that will spur massive internal migration.

And What Are the .01 Percenters Doing?

In the last decade, private land in the United States has become increasingly concentrated in the hands of a few. Today just 100 families own about 42 million acres across the country, a 65,000-square-mile expanse about the size of Wisconsin, according to the *Land Report*, a magazine that tracks large purchases.

The amount of land owned by those 100 families has jumped 50 percent since 2007 and 20 of the 100 families each owns more than 500,000 acres.

Very few of these enormous tracts are located in areas whose long-term value is made questionable by the warming. Those owners who have gone on record claim their purchases were for investment purposes—as hedges against the volatile markets. They are very well aware that, as a limited commodity, land is inherently valuable and will only become more so as the warming takes it away.

One also can't help but wonder if consideration isn't being given by some to converting these huge estates to secure and self-supporting refuges for themselves and their progeny.

Douglas Rushkoff in his new book, *Survival of the Richest: Escape Fantasies of the Tech Billionaires*, details the lengths to which the rich are trying to dodge the warming. For the wealthy, he says, the future of technology is about trying to escape from the rest of us.

For the wealthy and privileged, he says, the future of technology is about "only one thing: escape from the rest of us."

And they're escaping in style. Texas-based Rising S Company sells luxury bunkers that run up to $9.6 million for the Aristocrat Model—which comes with a private bowling alley, swimming pool, "bullet-resistant" doors and a "motor cave exit," so you can sneak out for errands like Batman.

In any case, as the Oklahoma Land Rush cheaters discovered, "sooner" in terms of relocation for the rest of us, will be better than "later."

This fictional vignette recounts an interview conducted in preparation for a news segment for the Environmental News Network.

Kent Whitaker Reporting
Off Key West, FL
Environmental News Network
April 2, 2034

THE SOLAR ARK

The small, rented 'copter hovered over a calm, azure Caribbean. Door off, Kent Whitaker's photographer, Jennifer Marson, legs dangling into the void, pointed her camera at the strangely beautiful vessel 500-feet below.

The M/V Solar Ark, a very large trimaran, was topped with a 50-foot "sail" rising from midship. The sail consisted of hundreds of high-performance solar panels arrayed on either side. Whitaker asked the pilot to circle slowly for photography and then request permission to land. He heard "roger that" in his headset.

With only the slightest bounce, the pilot put it down on the helipad's bullseye. Rotors folded, the ship's 'copter had been moved aside to a small parking area. Ship owner and designer Clarke Wilson, flowing white clothes flapping in the blades' dying downdraft, came out to meet them.

Wilson—white-haired, bearded, ruddy-complected—shook Whitaker's hand and led the two upstairs to a large, comfortably furnished room with a 180-degree view of the vessel and the sea beyond. Whitaker thought he looked like a prophet straight from the pages of the Bible.

"Welcome to the Ark," he smiled. "Thanks for your interest in our little venture."

Pleasantries over, Whitaker outlined his plan for the shoot. "First, I'd like to sit with you to get some background. Then, with your permission, we'd like a tour of the ship for some general shots."

As photographers do, Jen had already spotted an appropriate location for the interview. Moving away from the panoramic windows to eliminate hot backlighting, she pointed to comfortable leather chairs in front of a large painting of an eighteenth-century tall ship, cracking on in the dusk, its sails filled almost to bursting.

"Ah, good choice," Wilson said. "That's original artwork for the cover of one of Patrick O'Brian's 20 incredible volumes of historical fiction about the British navy." As he sat down, "I think I've read them four times…."

When Jen was ready: "Tell me about the ship. Talk as long as you like. We'll be editing the shoot to 4-5 minutes and it's always easier to have more to work with than less."

Wilson raised his arms and looked around. "This is the Wilson family's new home, including my kids and grandkids. Even my parents. Few are on board at the moment since this is a shakedown cruise. We're a pretty close-knit bunch and have decided to throw our lot in with the ocean instead of trying to fight it, as most everyone else seems to be doing. We've sold our homes, are moving on board and plan to cruise the world. That's not to say we'll never again set foot on *terra firma*. Of course we will. But this will be home."

"About the ship," Whitaker prodded.

"Yes, I've designed a vessel that's beyond state-of-the-art. The 175-foot Ark is a trimaran constructed of the latest polymers—lightweight, yet tough as a steel hull. It's powered by two 500-horsepower electric motors with solar energy provided by a unique solar-sail towering five stories above the main deck. Located on a moveable platform, the sail can be positioned to take best advantage of the sun. And, when wind conditions are right, the structure can also act as an actual sail.

"You might wonder if 1,000-horsepower is enough for a vessel of this size. While we certainly won't set any speed records, the Ark is light enough to cruise at a comfortable 12 knots. If necessary, we can run at 20 knots for several hours. Two large gyros keep the ship very steady, even in some relatively rough seas.

"I should also mention that the Ark is probably the most environmentally friendly ship ever built. Solar-power only. No fossil fuel on board for anything. Fresh water is provided by rain and our own desalination plant. Only readily biodegradable material goes into the water. That which is not biodegradable is bailed, stored and then put ashore for appropriate recycling."

"Can you explain the selection of the name? Sounds Biblical."

A smile wrinkled his face. "No, I'm not a Noah wannabe, though some say I look the part. And we're not going to be loading all animals two-by-two. Actually, my grandkids named it. Let's see. At last count, we're going to be home to three cats, two dogs, a pot-bellied pig, several tropical birds, an Iguana and at least one hamster. And who knows what else we might collect on the way. One granddaughter even suggested raising chickens for eggs. That idea was vetoed."

"What about crew?"

"We have a highly experienced captain with me acting as co-captain. A couple of mates, deckhands, cabin attendants and a chef. We also have a teacher and a formal classroom. We've had to disabuse the kids of visions of Huckleberry Finn."

"Sounds kind of crowded."

"Well, it'll be cozy. But we have comfortable crew's quarters, staterooms for the adults and bunkrooms for the kids. In addition, there's the great room in which we're sitting, dining room, two media rooms, exercise room and lap pool. Of course, we'll not always be on board. We'll stretch our legs at ports of call."

"What about dealing with hurricanes and the like?"

"Our plan is to cruise waters less inclined to rough weather. But it is a concern."

"Considering what's going on in the world, does this extravagant ocean-going home come with any pangs of guilt?"

Whitaker had forewarned Jen about the question and wanted an ECU.

"No, Mr. Whitaker. No guilt. Do I wish everyone had the resources I do? Certainly. Do some wealthy people deserve the label 'plutocrat?' Certainly. But I'm uncomfortable being tarred by the same brush. My grandfather made the family fortune in the rough and tumble world of manufacturing by producing products people wanted. In doing so, he created jobs for thousands. He paid his taxes without complaint. And never, to my knowledge, tried to buy politicians. He started the family foundation that, to date, has donated over $200 million to worthy causes.

"When he took the reins, my father sold off all our manufacturing businesses to focus on providing venture capital to Silicon Valley startups. He was responsible all or in part for a number of highly successful enterprises and further enhanced the family fortune.

"Me? I was able to start a successful maritime-design business. The boat you're floating on is the outcome of years of research and development. Is it merely an extravagance, an expression of my ego? I'd rather view it as a prototype, a testbed for systems that may be useful as we come to grips with surviving in an increasingly watery world.

"Now, shall we take a look around?"

Later, as the 'copter cruised toward its home base in Miami, Jen looked at Whitaker.

"I wish that pot-bellied pig had been on board," she said. The footage of 'Noah' was fine, but we could have used a little more fun."

Chapter Four
Inflation and the Dismal Science

"Dismal science" is a term coined by Scottish essayist and historian Thomas Carlyle to describe the discipline of economics. Dismal science is said to have been inspired by T.R. Malthus's gloomy prediction that population would always grow faster than food, dooming mankind to unending poverty and hardship.

In 1914, the exchange rate for the German Mark to the American dollar was 4.2 to one. Nine years later, following Germany's defeat in World War I, the exchange rate soared to 4.2 trillion to one. Waiters had to climb on tables every half hour to announce new menu prices. It is said that a loaf of bread cost a wheelbarrow full of marks. Many chose to avoid currency altogether, placing their faith in tangible assets to barter for goods.

Let's role play.

Imagine you're commuting to work. You overslept because—after punching the alarm—you rolled over for too many additional winks. Since you didn't have time to make coffee, you line up at a Starbuck's drive-through and order your favorite—a large mocha.

When you reach the pickup window, you realize you're short of cash. You hand over your debit card.

"Wow! Six bucks!" you think as you move ahead. "Well, I guess a treat once in a while is okay…."

As you pull onto the highway, your expenditure is deducted automatically from your account balance. Meanwhile, quietly and efficiently, other funds are flowing into and out of your account.

It's the first of the month and your two-week paycheck has just been directly deposited. The bank also withdrew your monthly mortgage payment—principle and interest with taxes and insurance directed to the appropriate escrow accounts. Other automatic withdrawals are scheduled for the day....

Back on the road, you tune into Public Radio. An economic report indicates inflation is running at over eight percent.

"Yeah, I can believe that!" you say, sipping your coffee.

The economist being interviewed expresses concern but says she views rising inflation as a temporary problem while the economy readjusts after COVID and supply chain issues. She says the economy is strong with unemployment and mortgage rates at historic lows.

"Maybe," you muse, "we should be looking more seriously for that bigger house."

You also reflect on your personal experience with the low unemployment rate. Your boss has been trying without success to hire someone to help you out. Basically, you've been doing two jobs for a couple of months.

On the way home you pull into your favorite ATM to get some cash for the weekend. At the end of the transaction, the machine dutifully reports your account balance, which reminds you that you need to review your credit card transactions this weekend and send in a couple of payments.

"Hate that job," you mutter. But paying on your credit cards is just about the only thing you won't entrust to automatic bill pay. You've suffered some credit card fraud in recent years. The credit card companies, of course, sent new cards right away and credited your account subject to an investigation.

"How much money do the credit card companies lose each year making good on fraud?" you wonder as you pull into your driveway....

It's unlikely this scenario in any way resembles a "typical" day for you—or anyone else for that matter. Let's view it instead as a composite picture consisting of elements of a typical day—yours and others.

The central point of the exercise is to remind us how transactional our lives are, how dependent we are on societal forces we can't control—the economy, for example—and how enmeshed we are in an electronic web that facilitates and abets our economic transactions and sometimes opens us up to scams and fraud.

A key question that the warming poses—one that will be the basis of this chapter and the next—is: "What's the future of money in an economy where high inflation is likely to become problematic? How will the warming affect how we transact the business of our lives?"

To Answer "Your" Question

Credit card companies are reluctant to divulge how much they lose each year to card fraud. But there are some amazing general statistics available:

- The U.S. economy, with the world's third highest rate of credit card fraud, suffered $34 billion in losses in 2022, up five percent from the previous year.

- Some 47 percent of Americans report having suffered credit card fraud in the last five years.

- In 2022, the Federal Trade Commission received more than 1.1 million reports of identity theft. The majority involved credit/debit card fraud.

Will there ever be a time in the U.S. when a loaf of bread will cost a wheelbarrow full of greenbacks as it did in post-WWI Germany?

Probably not.

Our fiscal system has built in mechanisms to control inflationary tendencies. But, as we should have learned by now, never say "never" in a world as complex and interdependent as ours has become.

Here's a brief tutorial on some aspects of the "dismal science" that apply. If you find your eyes glazing over, I can sympathize. But bear with me. I'll make this as painless as possible.

Let's briefly consider four types of inflation:

- **Creeping** or **Mild Inflation** occurs when prices rise by three percent or less per year. According to the Federal Reserve, price increases of two percent or less benefit economic growth. Mild inflation makes consumers expect that prices will keep going up, which boosts demand. For that reason, the Fed sets two percent as its target Core Inflation Rate (CIR).

- **Walking Inflation** is between 3-10 percent per year. It's harmful to the economy because it heats growth too quickly. People start to buy more than they need (i.e., hoarding) to avoid tomorrow's higher prices. This increased buying drives demand even further so that suppliers can't keep up. As supplies dwindle, prices rise even faster. As importantly, wages can't keep up. As a result, common goods and services may be priced out of reach for many people.

- **Galloping Inflation**—prices rising 10 percent or more in a year wreak havoc on an economy. Money loses value so quickly that business and employee income can't keep up with costs and prices. Foreign investors, in turn, avoid the country where this occurs, depriving it of needed capital. The economy becomes unstable, and the government loses credibility.

- **Hyperinflation** occurs when prices skyrocket by more than

20-30 percent per month. It's rare. Hyperinflation occurs when governments print too much money to pay for wars, civil unrest, economic mismanagement or corruption. It tends to occur during periods of economic and/or political turmoil. Examples include Germany in the 1920s and, most recently, Venezuela and Zimbabwe. (Zimbabwe printed a 100-trillion-dollar note in 2008, but it was not enough to buy a loaf of bread.) The first and last time the United States experienced hyperinflation was during the Civil War.

Getting a handle on inflation also requires some understanding of the concept of supply and demand—a model of markets that is probably the most famous contribution of economics to understanding forces at work in the marketplace.

Why is the law of supply and demand so powerful? The theory explains how demand and supply are connected and how these two behaviors strive to find market balance or equilibrium prices for goods and services. Usually when there is excess supply there is a decrease in price. Suppliers are willing to charge less to stimulate demand. Conversely, if supplies are limited consumers are willing to pay higher prices to secure what they need—to a certain point.

Thus, a major driver of inflation is limited supply. While suppliers work to offer consumers a sufficient supply of goods or services at prices they are willing or able to pay, unforecast variables can intervene. Good examples are inflation induced by COVID-related worker shortages and supply chain issues and the huge spike in gas prices resulting from the war in Ukraine.

The Federal Reserve prevents hyperinflation or other forms of inflation with monetary policy. The Fed's primary job is to control inflation while avoiding recession. It does this by tightening or relaxing the money supply—the amount of money allowed into the market—by adjusting its prime lending rate. Tightening the money supply reduces the risk of inflation while loosening it increases the risk.

The prime rate is used to set many interest rates such as those on credit cards, mortgages or business loans. Technically, there is no single U.S. prime rate. Banks set their own rates, but they generally move in lockstep with that established by The Fed.

As indicated, The Fed has a Core Inflation Rate target of two percent per year. But the CIR leaves out volatile oil and gas prices, commodities that move up and down rapidly depending on variables that affect commodities trading. Since fuel prices affect the price of food transported long distances, the Fed also removes food prices from the CIR.

In March, 2022, the U.S. CIR rose to 6.5 percent, the largest 12-month change since 1982.

But the CIR should not be confused with the Consumer Price Index (CPI). The CPI *does* include fuel and food costs, so it more accurately reflects what people buy and the impact of rising prices. The CPI had risen to 8.5 percent that month.

When you read this book, these figures will not be meaningful. They may be higher or lower depending on the interaction of determining variables at the time. I mention them only to indicate that, despite measures available to The Fed, inflation is difficult to control.

Thus, at one recent time (July, 2022), inflation could have been said to be "walking" very fast; even approaching "galloping" with prices going up at their fastest rate since the early 1980s.

Understanding money is tricky but necessary in considering possible financial scenarios created by the warming. It was much easier when we knew that five bucks in our wallet was backed by five bucks' worth of gold held in the U.S. Treasury. That was the "Gold Standard." But it was abolished in 1971 when Richard Nixon took us off the gold standard, replacing it with the "fiat system."

The term "fiat" is Latin for "let it be."

Thus, we are required to take the leap of faith that $5 is worth $5 because the government says so. For financial transactions to work, both seller and buyer must agree that the currency is worth its face value.

Until nations abandoned the gold standard—and all have—money, conceptually, was a simple matter. Paper currency was just a more convenient method to conduct transactions than to carry around a pocket or purse full of metallic coins. Prior to coinage, of course, buyers and sellers had to engage in the cumbersome process of bartering in transacting business.

Why, then, eliminate metallic-backed currency?

For one thing, there were concerns that the world's supply of gold was not sufficient to back all nations' currencies. As it turns out, that concern is no longer valid because of subsequent discoveries of large quantities of the precious metal.

More to the point, however, is the fact that the metallic standard means a government can't easily use monetary policy to manipulate its economy. Thus, the great benefit—and also a potential drawback—is that a government can arbitrarily and easily increase or decrease the supply of money as felt necessary to regulate its economy if it's not tied to a fixed supply of gold.

But here's where it really gets tricky. Currency must be considered, itself, to be a commodity governed by the law of supply and demand.

The demand for money tends to grow slowly over time. Growing economies produce more stuff so consumers demand more money—an increase in supply—with which to buy the stuff. There are three ways for a government to react:

- Increase the supply of money at the same rate as the growing demand. In this case prices don't change.
- Increase the supply faster than the demand. This makes money less valuable. Thus, prices increase, are inflated.
- Increase the supply slower than the demand. In this case,

money grows more valuable, reducing prices for goods or services—known as deflation.

So, the fiat system does allow for easy regulation of the economy. But why, then, is there the constant roller coaster from low to high inflation, from a relatively healthy to an unhealthy economy? The answer is—economies are highly complex and influenced by unforeseen variables, variables such as COVID, the war in Ukraine and, I'm suggesting, *the massive economic upheaval to be brought by the warming*.

The other scary aspect of the fiat system is that a government can, if it wishes, print as much money as it thinks necessary to pay extraordinarily high debts. Based on prior experience with hyperinflation, government economists know better. But that's today. Who knows what circumstances will be like 20-30 years from now when the warming's "bills" really start coming due?

As economist Sean Masaki Flynn put it, "The problem with the fiat money system is that nothing limits the number of little pieces of paper that the government can print to pay its debts."

Don't Bank on It!

For most of us, commercial banks have always been the center of our financial lives—the go-to place for almost anything having to do with money. What do you need? Checking or savings account? A mortgage, car or personal loan? Credit and debit card? Traveler's checks? Certified checks? Foreign currency? Safe deposit box?

The Federal Deposit Insurance Corporation (FDIC) indicates that there were over 4,200 commercial banks in the U.S in 2022 and they reported $279.1 billion in profits.

For the foreseeable future at least, banks should continue to be trustworthy places to help us conduct our financial lives. That is unless we should see another financial meltdown such as bedeviled the country—and the world—in 2007-2008.

The financial crisis began with cheap credit and lax lending standards that fueled a housing bubble. When the bubble burst, the banks were left holding trillions of dollars of worthless investments in subprime mortgages. (Subprime loans have interest rates that are higher than the prime rate and borrowers generally have low credit ratings.) The recession that followed cost many their jobs, their savings and homes.

It began, as usual, with good intentions. Faced with the bursting of the dot-com bubble, a series of corporate accounting scandals, and the September 11 terrorist attacks, the Federal Reserve lowered the prime rate from 6.5 percent in May 2000 to 1 percent in June 2003. The aim was to boost the economy by making money available to businesses and consumers at bargain rates.

Then greed raised its ugly head. (Remember Gordon Gecko's famous line in *Wall Street*? "Greed is good!")

The banks sold those subprime loans to Wall Street investment banks, which packaged them into what were billed as low-risk financial instruments. Soon a big secondary market for originating and distributing these worthless subprime loans developed.

For many Americans, their homes became worth less than they paid for them. They couldn't sell their houses without owing money to their lenders. If they had adjustable-rate mortgages, their costs were going up as their homes' values were going down. The most vulnerable subprime borrowers were stuck with mortgages they couldn't afford in the first place.

The economic damage and human suffering were immense. Unemployment reached 10 percent. About 3.8 million Americans lost their homes to foreclosures.

More than 500 banks failed between 2008 and 2015 compared to 25 in the preceding seven years. Most were small regional banks, and all were acquired by other banks, along with their depositors' accounts. But the biggest failures were not main street commercial banks but New York investment banks that catered to institutional investors.

Despite subsequent tightening of regulations, however, banks continue to fail. A recent example: In 2023, Silicon Valley Bank (SVB) failed after a bank run, *marking the third-largest bank failure in United States history and the largest since the 2007–2008 financial crisis.*

"SVB failed because of a textbook case of mismanagement by the bank. Its senior leadership failed to manage basic interest rate and liquidity risk. Its board of directors failed to oversee senior leadership and hold them accountable," according to the Federal Reserve.

But for now, banks are a pretty safe bet for your automatic withdrawals and deposits. And, as long as the FDIC continues to insure accounts up to $250,000, your deposits should be safe. But it is difficult to predict what the economic disruption caused by the warming will do to the banking system over time.

If greed continues to be good, I fear people may, at some point, need to start using The First Bank of Under-the-Mattress.

And there are other considerations. There have been over 200 recorded cyber incidents targeting financial institutions since 2007. In 2017, the G20 warned that cyberattacks could "undermine the security and confidence and endanger financial stability." (The G20 is a consortium of the world's largest economies.)

Déjà Vu (All Over Again!)

Of course, it's not only banks that are subject to the attacks of hackers both foreign and domestic.

In 2021, AT&T, that venerable communications company, suffered a massive data breach. In 2024, the same data set was re-exposed. The information of 73 million AT&T customers included names, addresses, phone numbers, and for some, Social Security numbers and birthdates. If exploited, cybercriminals can use this information to commit identity theft.

The telecommunications giant said that a dataset found on the "dark web" contains information for about 7.6 million current AT&T account holders and 65.4 million former account holders.

The obvious question, that, as of this writing, is unanswered—why didn't AT&T fix the problem after the first time around?

COVID could be viewed as a case history demonstrating how

sensitive to disruption our economy can be during times of stress.

The elevated inflation in 2022 was driven by supply chain disruptions and pent-up consumer demand for goods as the COVID-19 pandemic waned. The hope was that, should these issues resolve themselves, the Fed might not have as much work to do on the inflation front.

But, just as COVID lingered, it looked more and more likely that high inflation would also linger. In the 12-month period ending in March, 2022, energy prices had risen 32 percent and the food index increased by 8.8 percent, the largest 12-month increase since the period ending May, 1981. Shelter costs also contributed to the near galloping inflation, rising five percent during the same period.

Energy prices, of course, were also affected early in 2022 by the war in Ukraine—just another example of how unanticipated global events have repercussions on the U.S. economy.

The point of this mini-case history is simple. If a pandemic and a war in Europe affect our economy to this extent, imagine the ways in which a never-ending and ever-worsening global catastrophe like the warming will wreak economic havoc.

And the Forecast Is....

Have you heard this one? In what profession can practitioners be wrong 80 percent of the time, but still keep their jobs? The answer: Meteorology. Funny? Yes. But accurate? No. Even though we're all accustomed to having unforecast rain fall on the occasional parade, the fact is that a seven-day forecast can accurately predict the weather about 80 percent of the time; a five-day forecast, approximately 90 percent. A 10-day—or longer—forecast, is only right about half the time.

There is one profession, however, whose forecasting ability is even more suspect. *Economics.*

Prakash Loungani at the International Monetary Fund (IMF) analyzed the accuracy of economic forecasters and found something remarkable and worrying. "The record of failure to predict recessions is virtually unblemished," he said.

His analysis revealed that economists failed to predict 148 of the past 150 recessions. Part of the problem, he said, was that there isn't much reputational gain to be had by predicting a recession others had missed. If you disagreed with the consensus, you would be met with skepticism. The downside of getting it wrong was more personally damaging than the upside of getting it right.

"Not only have we been bad at forecasting, but there is not much sign of improvement." According to Mark Pearson, Organization for Economic Cooperation and Development (OECD), "We are getting worse at making forecasts because the world is getting more complicated."

Increased complexity is not the only problem—forecasts are also made less trustworthy because of a feedback loop. If a meteorologist says it will rain, the fact that you take an umbrella out with you does not affect the weather. But if an economist forecasts that inflation will rise by three percent and we react by asking for at least a three percent rise in wages, we have changed the basis on which the forecast was made. Inflation is now likely to rise by more than three percent. The fact that the forecast exists changes the reality it is trying to predict.

Chapter Five
Economic *Quid Quo Pro*

*"Give me one of yours And I'll give
you one of mine. Is that fair and square?"*
—Lorin R. Robinson

What, then, is the future of money, of currency, in an economy that will soon be battered by the massive disruptions and uncertainties generated by the warming. How will Americans manage their financial lives in an economy that will likely increasingly be characterized by scarcity and the inflation that will result?

Considering the complexity and interdependence of today's world, it would be foolish for anyone to claim the ability to predict with any precision the medium and, certainly, the long-term impact of the warming on the economic lives of people as they confront the upheavals it will bring.

But fools rush in.

At some point within several decades, many Americans may be required to ask and answer financial questions they've never before confronted. How will people obtain goods and services they require using inflated currency resulting in prices too high to pay? How will people afford food, housing, fuel and to pay for all the other myriad expenses of daily living when incomes have not kept up with inflation and unemployment is high? Or, worse, how can people survive in an economy whose currency has simply collapsed and has no value?

Do I overstate? Am I really just a conspiracist in journalist's clothing?

Remember. This is a thought exercise in which we are considering possibilities. And the scenario just described is certainly within the realm of possible warming-induced economic outcomes.

Several factors support such a dire view. One is inflation. Another is high unemployment—a subject to be dealt with in a succeeding chapter. Still another is the unknown and probably unknowable costs of constantly battling the impact of hurricanes, coastal inundation, flooding, fires and other climatic catastrophes destroying the homes in which we live, the businesses in which we work and our nation's infrastructure.

And one can't forget the fragile and hackable nature of the Internet upon which our financial institutions and we, their customers, rely.

As you will remember, inflation is a creature of scarcity. The less there is of something or somethings, the more it or they will cost. And, as will be demonstrated in subsequent chapters—to paraphrase *Game of Thrones*—scarcity is coming.

Food Scarcity—A Preview

Chapter Seven will deal in depth with the impact of the warming on the availability of food. As indicated earlier, increasing temperatures are resulting in prolonged drought, desertification and water shortages both here are around the world. All three factors, obviously, have a major impact on agriculture.

But it's not all about daily high temperatures.

In California's highly agricultural Central Valley, wintertime lows have gotten warmer. This is critical because the perennial crops comprising the bulk of California's top farm commodities need off-season dormancy to regenerate. So, temperatures must remain below a certain threshold for at least a minimum amount of time in a growing season, a concept called "chill hours."

California provides more agricultural products than any other state, accounting for 11 percent of the national total. That output includes more than two-thirds of the nation's fruits and nuts and more than one-third of our vegetables.

California's top 10 agricultural commodities among its more than 400, in order, are—dairy products, almonds, grapes, pistachios, cattle, lettuce, strawberries, tomatoes, floriculture and walnuts.

Excluding animal products, these are primarily perennials needing—but increasingly not getting—the chill hours required to grow successfully.

Fruit such as apples, cherries and pears need chill hours of at least 1,000 hours and were already barely suited to Central Valley conditions 20 years ago. It's projected that more than half of the Central Valley will no longer be suitable for growing crops like apricots, peaches, plums and walnuts sometime around the middle of the century.

Another major factor contributing to coming economic instability is the financial toll on the national economy of adapting to the ever-worsening climate and repairing the incessant damage to the infrastructure that provides the backbone of our civilization—roads, bridges, railroads, airports, ports, utilities and more.

That's the big picture. But one must also include the impact of the warming's mischief on the many millions whose homes, businesses and places of work will be damaged or destroyed by coastal inundation, flooding, hurricanes, tornadoes, wildfires....

Keeping the Country Running—A Preview

Chapter Nine will take a detailed look at the coming degradation of our infrastructure—focusing primarily on energy—and what may be the unbearably high cost of keeping the country functioning.

While the future is uncertain, the past is not.

According to NOAA, the cumulative costs of the 16 separate billion-dollar weather events in the U.S. in 2017 was $306.2 billion, breaking the previous cost record of $214.8 billion (2005). It is estimated that Hurricane Harvey alone had total costs of $125 billion—second only to Hurricane Katrina which had an approximate cost of $160 billion.

But do these figures tell the whole tale?

Unfortunately, there is no standard or agreed upon method for calculating the true cost of a weather event such as a hurricane. Figures given are often misleading since they may include only losses that were *greater* than insured losses (i.e., not covered by insurance). Widely reported damages caused by Ida in 2021, for example, were $60-65 billion. But catastrophe risk-modeler RMS has estimated that insured losses from Ida could reach $40 billion, making its true cost closer to $100 billion.

As the warming continues to wind up, the cost of damage to our infrastructure will escalate into the trillions annually.

So, what is the answer to the question with which the chapter opened? What is the future of money, of currency, in an economy that will increasingly be battered by the massive disruptions and uncertainties generated by the warming? How will Americans manage their financial lives in an economy that will likely be characterized by scarcity and the inflation that will result?

In short, how will we go about the business of living?

The answer, or at least a partial answer, may seem ludicrous or outlandish considering the fact that today, on the world stage, America is the ultimate land of plenty with the world's biggest economy. Inflation, while higher as of this writing than desired, is usually kept in check. Employment is high with many businesses going begging for employees. And now that the COVID – supply chain hiccough has improved, goods are generally plentiful.

But the warming will ensure that, over the coming decades, this bubble will burst.

And the answer is? (After all the buildup, a drum roll here would be nice.) The answer, in large measure, may be *bartering*—a form of economic *quid quo pro*.

Quid quo pro—a Latin term translated as "something for something"—originated in the Middle Ages and can describe a situation in which two parties engage in a mutual agreement to exchange goods or services reciprocally—without the use of currency.

It's a fancy term for bartering.

Bartering is the act of trading one good or service for another without using a medium of exchange such as money. A bartering economy differs from a monetary economy in several ways. The primary difference is that goods or services are exchanged immediately, and the exchange is reciprocal. It's a negotiation in which barterers get what they want in what they perceive to be an even exchange in terms of value.

Bartering, of course, is an ancient practice that preceded the advent of money around 600 BC. The first industrial facility to manufacture coins that could be used as currency is reputed to have been located in a region called Lydia in modern-day Western Turkey. The Chinese were the first to devise a system of paper money, in approximately 770 BC.

Prior to the invention and gradual adoption of currency around the world, people traded for what they needed and were often participants in relatively large and complex trading networks.

This is not to say that currencies of sorts weren't used earlier. It wasn't always an exchange of commodities. Certain rare items such as precious or semi-precious stones, metals—even shells known as cowries—were employed. But they weren't used universally within a given population and their values were difficult to determine.

Today, in times of monetary crisis or collapse, a bartering system often becomes a major means to continue the exchange of goods and services. To survive Venezuela's hyperinflation, for example, many people have simply abandoned the country's currency and taken to using the Bolivar as wallpaper.

In 2021, Venezuela released a new currency that features six fewer zeros, a response to years of hyperinflation. The highest denomination of the Venezuelan currency had previously been a one-million Bolivar note, worth a little less than $0.25. That has become a one Bolivar note.

As a substitute for currency, bartering has both advantages and disadvantages. In an economy that's working more-or-less well, the disadvantages significantly outweigh the advantages because it is so much easier simply to run your credit card than to navigate the several steps involved in completing a successful bartering transaction:

- Barterers need to have something of value to trade.
- Barterers must find others who are interested in what they have to offer and have what they need in return.
- A third critical step involves reaching agreement as to the respective value of the items. Can both parties to the transaction feel they've gotten a good deal?

Obviously, bartering requires a great deal of commitment, particularly if it's a primary means in which basic needs are being satisfied. But all sorts of necessary commodities can be obtained through trade—food, clothing, household items, fuel, tools and building materials are just a few examples.

Of course, bartering isn't limited only to tangible items. Services are also bartered. It wasn't uncommon, for example, for a doctor during the Depression to make a house call, stitch up a wound, and receive a freshly plucked chicken in recompense. Actually, almost any service or skill is barterable:

- Service providers can be compensated for work with tangible goods.
- Services can also be bartered for services. An electrician and a plumber might, for example, swap labor on each other's home construction projects.

It's not widely realized, but millions of Americans today are barterers. Person-to-person bartering is facilitated by Craigslist, Facebook Marketplace, co-ops, flea markets and swap meets. There are also sophisticated barter exchange websites that enable members—people and businesses alike—to trade goods or services.

Looking further ahead, though, bartering will probably be accomplished most efficiently within local networks of friends and bartering partners. It will also be advantageous to have a readily and easily barterable skill set and/or commodity that can be offered in trade.

Warren Buffet on Bartering

"The best thing you can do is to be exceptionally good at something. If you're the best doctor in town, if you're the best lawyer in town, if you're the best whatever it may be... [people] are going to give you some of what they produce in exchange for what you deliver.

"Whatever abilities you have can't be taken away from you. So, the best investment by far is anything that develops you...."

Buffett emphasizes that sharpening one's skills and working to be the top of one's field is inflation proof.

"No matter what the dollar is worth, if an individual has a skill that is in high demand, unlike a currency, the skill will continue to be in high demand."

According to prepper blogger Dan "Survival" Sullivan, "bartering is going to be one of those skills that will almost guarantee that you and your family will not only survive but thrive in a post-apocalyptic world." According to Sullivan, one of the most dreaded things after an SHTF ("Shit Hits the Fan") Event will be the uselessness of money.

"After an economic collapse or some other catastrophe, the banking system is going to be seriously crippled. Cash in hand is going to be pretty much useless.... Everyone will want the physical items that will help them survive," Sullivan says.

SHTF Event?

In case you missed it in the "Grim Glossary" in front of the book, preppers define an SHTF Event as one that is extremely disruptive, one in which government efforts at containment either do no good or make things worse, one in which people are no longer guaranteed access to survival necessities like food, water and shelter. And the warming is going to be the mother of all SHTF Events.

Are there other alternative methods to cope with the high inflation that will undoubtedly accompany the warming as it evolves over the next several decades? Some might suggest the use of gold in place of currency. "Goldbugs"—those who advocate investing in gold instead of or in addition to other investment alternatives—may be heard to claim that "gold can be used as a hedge against inflation."

Don't be misled, however. Gold may or may not be a good investment strategy compared to stocks or bonds—and the jury is out on this point—but it offers no benefit in replacing currency in the day-to-day financial transactions in which we all engage.

Simple example. Let's say the price of a loaf of bread at your local grocery store is $5. You could hand the cashier a $5 gold coin instead of an equal amount of paper currency and, while the transaction today would be unusual and might require the clerk to consult with the manager, you'd leave the store with your bread.

If several years (or months) later the price of that loaf of bread has risen to $10, you'd have to fork over a $10 gold coin to conclude the transaction. As currency, gold does not offer any "hedge against inflation."

On the Streets of Moscow

I've had only limited experience with bartering. But, thinking back, there was one....

In the mid-80s, while a journalism professor, I led a group of students to the Soviet Union to compare our two distinctly different approaches to "news." I had a few minutes to myself one day between visits to the news agency Tass and newspaper *Pravda*. So, I roamed the streets of Moscow with my camera.

At one point a young man sidled up to me and, in good English, complimented me on my telephoto lens. "I have a Pentax, but I do not have a telephoto. Would you like to trade something for it?"

I knew the black market was alive and well there at the time, so my first inclination was to decline. The last thing I needed to do was to be caught in a sting operation. But, intrigued, I said, "What do you have?"

"Well," he said, "if you'll come to my apartment, I'm sure we can find something you'd like. It's very close."

More red flags. What if I were being set up to be robbed? Or held hostage? Nonetheless, I agreed, and we walked about five minutes to a depressing Soviet-style apartment block. His unit, which was a few flights up, turned out to be more like a small warehouse. Clearly, I had walked into the den of a serious trader.

As we threaded a narrow path between TV sets, audio equipment and small appliances—some boxed, some not—he turned to me. "What about a nice Sony boom box?" He smiled broadly at his little joke, knowing full well it was not something I could easily carry home.

We finally came to a table on which were displayed a number of black enamel boxes, each bearing an exquisitely painted Russian folk tale in miniature. I knew they were worth hundreds since I had seen them displayed in the tourist-only (foreign currency) *beriozka* stores.

He handed me a large one. "What about this?"

I hesitated, not believing my good fortune. The box was worth so much more than my old 200 mm lens. He must have taken my hesitation to be a bargaining tactic. He handed me a second smaller one.

I unhooked my lens and handed it to him. He seemed genuinely pleased.

"*Spacibo*," (thank you), I said, using one of the few Russian words

I knew. *"Pojaluista,"* (you're welcome), he said as he escorted me to the door.

That was 1984. Today I'm certain bartering and the black market are still mainstays of Russia's dysfunctional economy. With Putin's war on Ukraine and the resulting economic sanctions, inflation is rampant. Russian inflation accelerated to 23.7 percent in 2022, its highest since 1999.

I know it's difficult to wrap one's head around the idea that bartering may become a survival mainstay in the coming world of the warming. Accepting the idea requires accepting the notion mentioned earlier that people are simply going to have to lower their expectations.

At the risk of being repetitious:

There is going to be the pressing need to readjust our expectations—our lifestyles—in order to cope with growing limitations imposed by the warming. There will be the need for people to accept—even embrace—simplicity, self-reliance and sustainability in how they organize their lives to survive in what will be a very different world.

Chapter Six
America on the Move

"Choking on the dust,
The Okies fled west to Eden
There to be reviled."
—Lorin R. Robinson

The last and only other time adverse climatic conditions forced a massive migration in America was in the 1930s—the Dust Bowl. Driven by the depression, drought and dust, thousands left their homes in Oklahoma, Texas, Arkansas and Missouri. The exact number of Dust Bowl refugees remains a matter of controversy, but, by some estimates, as many as 400,000 migrants headed west to California.

The "Okies," as they were known generically, were not welcomed in California.

Though the U.S. is among the most technologically advanced nations in the world and boasts its biggest economy, warming-induced migration is inevitable. As noted in an earlier chapter, about 127 million Americans—almost 40 percent of the population—live in ocean-side counties. Though these counties encompass only 10 percent of the country's land mass, in aggregate they have a GDP that would make them the third largest economy in the world.

By 2050 the disruption caused by ocean inundation, flooding and devastating weather will have driven millions in these counties from their homes. Increasing temperatures, humidity and drought will also drive millions more from the Southeast, Deep South and Southwest. The likely destinations? As meteorological modeling cited earlier indicates—the Northwest, northern Rocky Mountain States, northern Upper Midwest and north and northeastward of the Ohio Valley.

What will be the economic and social impact of this dislocation—on individuals, families and the regions from which and to which they fled?

Let's consider real estate and the inexorable law of supply and demand. As a region loses population through migration, property values will decrease. Many homeowners, for example, may be underwater—if not literally, then figuratively. They may need to sell at a loss if they can sell at all. That's why I cautioned earlier that it will be better to be a "sooner" rather than a "later" in making warming-based relocation decisions.

Meanwhile, at the destination end, migrants face another problem—the likelihood of housing shortages and ever-increasing property values. The cost of renting will also be inflated.

Migration will have other devastating effects on the economies of both the sending and receiving areas.

Out-migration will leave unemployment in its wake. The retail, service and entertainment sectors, in particular, will suffer through loss of business. School systems, hospitals and governmental agencies will have to downsize, leading to further unemployment. The tax base will dwindle as people and businesses leave the area, resulting in ever less revenue to pay for services and to clean up from devastating weather-related events.

And the opposite will be true on the receiving end. Unemployment should be reduced initially, but the time may come when in-migration exceeds employment needs. Demand for schools, medical care and governmental assistance may exceed available resources. Meanwhile, increased demand for goods and services will probably result in high regional inflation. The influx of migrants, many of whom will not come with or find jobs, will lead to taxation deficits that adversely affect funding for schools and governmental services.

Will the warming migrants receive the same kind of welcome the Okies received in California in the 1930s?

As the warming continues to warm, hundreds of millions of people around world will also be on the move, seeking shelter from increasing temperatures, water shortages, rising oceans, catastrophic weather and political upheaval. This migration is already underway and will accelerate in years and decades to come.

One of the most contentious political issues in the U.S. for decades has revolved around how to handle the millions of Mexican and Central American would-be immigrants seeking to enter the country legally or illegally.

In 2023, more than 2.4 million encounters with migrants at the border were reported by U.S. Customs and Border Protection. In addition to Mexican citizens, many were from Central American countries—primarily El Salvador, Guatemala, Honduras and Nicaragua.

The warming will only fuel this controversy for the U.S. as it will for other countries that might offer a safe or safer haven for those—particularly those living inside the Tropics of Capricorn and Cancer—trying to escape extremes of temperature, drought, disease, food and water shortages.

In Mexico, for example, drought and desertification are forecast to lead to a 40-70 percent decline in the country's current cropland suitability by 2030. Worse, this could soar to an 80-100 percent decline by the end of the century. We're talking about Mexico potentially losing over half its workable farms in less than 10 years and all of them by 2100.

Hurricanes Eta and Iota struck Central America in November, 2020 as Category 4 hurricanes bringing torrential rain, flash floods, landslides and crop damage across Honduras, El Salvador,

Guatemala and Nicaragua. The UN estimates that 7.3 million people in the region were affected by the twin storms, leading to increased migration.

According to a CNBC report, "The impact of the hurricanes is one of many reasons migrants from Central America are making the dangerous journey to the U.S. southern border to seek refuge—and just one example of climate-exacerbated drivers of displacement and migration."

It is ironic that, as many Americans will eventually migrate north to escape the increasingly inhospitable lands in the lower half of the country, millions from climate-devastated countries to our south will seek to enter those lands as "climate refugees" for whom the conditions would be an improvement.

This fictional television report suggests a likely reaction of U.S. states faced with substantial and sustained in-migration as the warming worsens. Camera directions are provided but may be ignored in favor of just reading the narrative.

Kent Whitaker Reporting
Environmental News Network
January 14, 2034, 6:15 p.m. CST

MINNESOTA NICE

Anchor, Medum Close Up (MCU): We're back and have Senior Editor Kent Whitaker with us reporting from St. Paul, Minnesota. Kent, are you as miserable as you look?

Cut to Whitaker MCU Stand Upper

Whitaker: Absolutely. I think I'm too old for stand-uppers—particularly when the temp is below freezing with wind chills around minus 20. While I appreciate our new ENN parkas, I think they need a few more pounds of insulation. The Upper Midwest is in the grips of its least favorite weather pattern. The polar vortex has sagged south for an extended period, again wrapping its arms around the country's upper midsection. But this, of course, is not a weather forecast. We leave those to our sister net, The Weather Channel.

Camera One slow zoom to Long Shot (LS)

Whitaker: Behind me is the Minnesota State Capitol where the House just approved a controversial bill designed to stem the rising tide of emigration to Minnesota from areas of the country suffering from the warming. Say what you will about Minnesota winters, at least the state has water, moderate temperatures and suffers less from destructive weather.

Camera cut to B-roll (video) of House Chambers

Whitaker Voice Over (VO): The bill—which passed in the House by a substantial margin—would make it difficult for new residents to access the state's welfare system and for their children to attend public schools. Those seeking to move to Minnesota would have to apply for permission. Particularly controversial is a provision allowing police to stop vehicles with out-of-state license plates in order to determine residency. Those not on a list of approved new residents would be required to appear in court to give cause as to why they should not be required to leave the state. The bill has been passed on to the Senate for deliberation and ratification. If approved, Governor Mel Johnson says he will sign it. Earlier I talked with the bill's house sponsor—Representative Thorvald "Thor" Thorssen.

Cut to Video

Camera One to Whitaker Close Up (CU)

Whitaker: Representative Thorssen, considering Minnesota's long-standing heritage as a liberal state—the state of Hubert Humphrey, Walter Mondale and others, doesn't your bill, which some have termed unconstitutional, seem out of step?

Camera Two cut to Thorssen CU

Thorssen: Yes, we've had our liberals over the years. But there are those—and I am one of them—who don't believe liberalism has served us well. In any case, times change. Given the current situation, I'm not at all sure a Humphrey or a Mondale would disagree with this legislation.

Camera One cut to Whitaker CU

Whitaker: What, specifically, led you to introduce this bill?

Camera Two cut to Thorssen MCU over Whitaker's shoulder

Thorssen: I brought this idea to the House seven years ago when I first took office. No one took me seriously. But, as I said, times change. In the past 10 years, Minnesota has absorbed almost three million new residents and grown from seven million to some 10 million. Many of these new residents came without jobs and without financial resources.

Camera One cut to Whitaker CU reaction shot

Thorssen (VO): The strain on our—to my mind—overly generous welfare system, our public schools, medical facilities, law enforcement and infrastructure are bankrupting the state. Our taxpayers are being asked to pick up the bill. I know this makes us look like we don't care. We do. But, as legislators, it's our job to protect the health, well-being and way of life of our constituents.

Camera One stay on Whitaker CU

Whitaker: What criteria are applied to those who would be acceptable and those who would not?

Camera Two cut to Thorssen CU

Thorssen: First and foremost, they'd have to demonstrate that they either have a job in Minnesota or have sufficient other resources to support themselves. In other words, will they be Minnesota taxpayers? Our welfare system, public schools, public health care facilities and other state-supported services will not be available to anyone not meeting that basic requirement.

Camera One cut to Whitaker CU

Whitaker: And what about police stops of vehicles with out-of-state plates? Is that even constitutional?

Camera Two cut to Thorssen MCU over Whitaker's shoulder

Thorssen: We believe an out-of-state plate is sufficient probable cause to suspect the driver does not have a Minnesota driver's license and—unless the driver can prove he or she is in transit—is not among those legally granted residence. Incidentally, if the Senate approves the bill and it's signed into law, we fully expect a Supreme Court challenge. However, we've done our homework and believe there's nothing in the bill prohibited by the Constitution. States, Mr. Whitaker, still have rights and we intend to exercise ours.

Camera One cut to Whitaker CU

Whitaker: If the bill is approved—and survives a court test—do you think other states in similar situations will follow suit?

Camera Two cut to Thorssen CU

Thorssen: Delegations from several states have visited with us and are tracking our progress. They, of course, would prefer that we not name them. But, yes, I think our legislation might serve as a prototype.

End video, cut to Whitaker stand upper

Whitaker (MCU): Anne, I'd be inclined to say we're witnessing the end of "Minnesota Nice." But states like Minnesota have a legitimate problem. While this solution certainly would not be welcomed by those needing to relocate, it may become a fact of life. Wasn't it Minnesotan Bob Dylan who back in the '60s warned that times are changing? How right he was.

Cut to Anchor: Thanks, Kent. Now, get thee to a hot toddy.

Cut to commercial

Chapter Seven
The Future of Food

"The Day will come when we will wonder what happened to all those ceiling – tall cereal shelfs at the grocery store. Oh well, I never trusted cereals that turned my milk some color...."
—Lorin R. Robinson

One needn't be familiar with Maslow's Hierarchy of Needs to know that, in addition to water and shelter, food is a primary prerequisite for life. Unfortunately for many, in the coming world of the warming, access to sufficient calories for survival will become a challenge.

According to the U.S. Department of Agriculture, people need about 2,500 calories daily to maintain good health and appropriate weight. The UN World Health Organization (WHO) sets the minimum calorie target at 1,800. The Harvard Medical School differentiates by gender and sets minimum caloric intake per day at 1,200 for women and 1,800 for men.

It is generally agreed that starvation occurs with a caloric intake of fewer than 600 calories per day; however, any intake below the recommended minimums doesn't provide the body with the fuel it needs to function properly.

It should come as no surprise that Americans lead the world in daily caloric consumption, averaging about 3,500. At the bottom of the global list is the Democratic Republic of the Congo where people average far less than half—1,590 calories.

Diet Anyone?

Obesity costs the United States about $150 billion a year, or almost 10 percent of the national medical budget. Approximately one in three adults and one in six children is obese. Obesity is considered to be an epidemic and a major cause of deaths attributable to heart disease, cancer and diabetes.

And what's driving America's chronic weight problem? The preponderance of evidence points to causes most people already suspect—too much food, too much food with too little nutritional value and too little exercise.

Food security, as defined by the United Nations' Committee on World Food Security, means that "all people, at all times, have physical, social, and economic access to sufficient, safe and nutritious food that meets their food preferences and dietary needs for an active and healthy life."

But food *insecurity*—both moderate and severe—has consistently increased worldwide since 2014, when the prevalence of under-nourishment was at 8.6 percent. It's now at 8.9 percent. *That's almost 700 million people.* Between 2018 and 2019, the number of hungry people grew by 10 million. If the trend continues, the number could reach 840 million by 2030.

The majority of this increase has come from Asia, where most undernourished people live—some 381 million. But Africa's hungry population is the fastest growing and currently stands at about 250 million. Global population growth, obviously, is a contributor.

Malnourished, Undernourished, Overnourished

Malnutrition is defined as deficiencies, imbalances, or excesses in a person's dietary intake. It's affected by the quantity but also the quality of diets.

How can excess nutrition be a form of malnutrition? The answer is *overnutrition* caused by an excess of nutrients, mainly calories, and a cause of obesity that can result in ailments such as diabetes and cardiovascular diseases.

Oddly, just as the world's getting hungrier, every world region is also becoming more overweight. However, the UN Food and Agriculture Organization (FAO) cautions that this should not be confused with improved nutrition. Food insecurity often results from poor empty-calorie diets that lead to weight gain.

Undernutrition is caused by not having enough to eat or having a diet that lacks proper nutrition—calories, protein or other vital vitamins and minerals. This is type of malnutrition leads to low weight-for-height (wasting), low height-for-age (stunting) and low weight-for-age (underweight), particularly in children. Undernutrition is a result of low quantity and poor quality of food.

The UN's goal has been complete eradication of world hunger by 2030, but the organization now readily admits that the goal is unrealistic. Its World Food Program (WFP) predicted a global food "catastrophe" in a report released in 2022.

Up to 2.3 billion people faced moderate to severe food insecurity in 2021, with those numbers only projected to rise, according to the report. WFP blamed global conflict, the COVID-19 pandemic and climate change for exacerbating hunger levels across the globe. Countries in Central America, Africa and the Middle East will endure the severest shortages, the report predicts.

The report found that the total number of people nearing *starvation-level hunger* rose from some 276 million before Russia invaded Ukraine to about 345 million as of June, 2022. Prior to the onset of the COVID-19 pandemic, that number was at just around 135 million.

"The result (of food insecurity) will be global destabilization, starvation and mass migration on an unprecedented scale. We have to act today to avert this looming catastrophe," said David Beasley, director of the WFP.

The Warming-Generated Genocide in Darfur

Conflict between African farmers and Arab nomadic tribes first arose in the 1980s in the Darfur Region of Sudan as drought and famine spread throughout the area. Tribes began to fight each other as usable land became a precious commodity. Most disputes were settled by local, democratic councils using non-violent intervention.

But in 1989 the National Islamic Front (NIF) seized control in Sudan and tensions among the African farmers and the Arab nomadic tribes increased. The local governments were disempowered and the NIF favored Arab tribes over the Africans. Violent conflicts continued to escalate, and areas became increasingly divided by ethnicity and economic status.

In 2003, the Justice and Equality Movement (JEM) and the Sudan Liberation Army (SLA) rebelled against the Sudanese government, claiming that the government was ethnically cleansing all Africans out of Darfur. In an attempt to crush these rebel groups, the NIF armed and paid various militant groups to obliterate the JEM and SLA, as well as thousands of innocent people.

The most infamous of these militias is the *Janjaweed*. It is responsible for deaths, rapes and displacement of almost 2.7 million people. It burned and bombed villages, took or killed livestock, destroyed crops, and poisoned water so it's impossible for victims to return.

Human conflict goes hand-in-hand with food supply issues, cautions Peter deMenocal, president and director, Woods Hole Oceanographic Institute.

"With food insecurity comes human conflict," he says. "This is something that's been well documented both in the prehistorical record but also in the recent historical record such as Syria and, of course, migrations out of North Africa into Europe. When people are hungry, they migrate, and they'll migrate to places where there's food, which is typically the wealthier nations."

He warns that this migration can lead to political instability and says these types of geopolitical concerns are monitored not only by climate modelers and researchers, but also by government intelligence agencies seeking to anticipate and mitigate conflicts.

Clearly, over the coming decades, a changing climate, a growing global population, rising food prices, environmental stressors and global conflict will have a significant yet uncertain effect on food security.

Meanwhile, in the United States....

According to the USDA, 38.3 million people in the U.S. lived in food-insecure households in 2020. Of these, 6.1 million were children.

"COVID has just wreaked havoc on so many things: on public health, on economic stability and obviously on food insecurity," said Luis Guardia, the president of the Food, Research and Action Center.

But, even before the pandemic hit, some 13.7 million U.S. households (10.5 percent) experienced food insecurity at some point during 2019, according to the USDA. These Americans were either unable to acquire enough food to meet their needs or were uncertain from where their next meal might come.

In 2015, undernourishment—an extreme form of food insecurity—was reported to afflict 2.5 percent of the U.S. population—about eight million people. Of those, some 200,000 were children under five.

The official poverty rate in 2020 was 11.4 percent, according to the U.S. Census. This means that 11.4 percent of Americans were living below the federally determined poverty threshold. This percentage was up from 10.5 percent in 2019 and was the first increase in five years.

As indicated, the USDA estimates that 38.3 million Americans suffered food insecurity in 2020. That's 11.6 percent—*a figure eerily but not unexpectedly close to the percentage living under the poverty ceiling.*

In a strange twist, however, living with food insecurity does not necessarily mean low-income Americans escape the possibility of being overweight. Their diets tend to be high in calories but low in nutritional value, leading both to obesity and nutritional deficiencies.

But obesity and poor nutrition are not limited to low-income Americans. The prevalence of obesity in the U.S. population as a whole is 42 percent. According to a 2016 listing, America is the 12th most obese country in the world. The first other so-called developed nation to appear on the list is Canada at number 26.

This Is SAD

A dietary quality index, which ranks the quality of diets on a scale of 0-100, places what's known as the Standard American Diet (SAD) at 11. The higher the score, the more body fat people tend to lose over time and the lower their obesity, blood pressure, cholesterol and triglycerides. *Sadly, it appears most Americans—poor or not—hardly make it past a score of 10 on this 0-100 scale.*

According to the USDA, the SAD consists of 32 percent of calories derived from animal foods, 57 percent from processed plant foods, and only 11 percent from whole grains, beans, fruits, vegetables and nuts.

If you waded through all those statistics, thanks for sticking with me. They did have a purpose.

Clearly, the world is already facing a severe food insecurity problem that will only worsen dramatically as the climate-changing effects of the warming become more pronounced. And the United States—ostensibly the world's richest country—is actually, on average, less well off in terms of food security than the rest of the world. In 2019, before the pandemic, an estimated 10.5 percent of Americans were food insecure. *The world average was 8.9 percent!*

In terms of food, the warming is a recipe for disaster. As has already been suggested, warming-caused modifications of the climate will severely strain our ability to grow essential crops and raise livestock. The culprits, of course, are the ever-increasing average global temperatures and reduced or, at best, erratic delivery of moisture—rainfall and snow. Increasing and increasingly violent weather events and coastal flooding also play a role.

Temperature rise and reduced moisture are producing unprecedented drought and desertification around the world and in the U.S., already reducing the amount of viable agricultural land. Here are just a few alarming examples:

- A dramatic drying trend in 2021 pushed a 22-year drought in the U.S. past the previous records and shows no signs of easing. This mega-drought deepened so much recently that it is has been ranked the most severe in at least 1,200 years.

- The climate crisis is reducing consumable food calories worldwide by around one percent yearly for the top 10 global crops. This may sound small, but it represents some 35 trillion calories each year—enough to provide more than 50 million people with a daily diet of over 1,800 calories—the level that the UN identifies as essential to "avoid food deprivation or undernourishment."

- It is estimated that each decade of warming will decrease the amount of food the world can produce by two percent, or 4.4 million tons.

- Climatic changes will also drive-up food prices. A 2021 study predicts that by 2040 food prices will be four times higher than they were in 2000. They're already twice as high as they were then.

- By 2070, extremely hot zones like the Sahara that now cover less than one percent of the earth's land surface, could cover nearly a fifth, potentially placing one of every three people alive outside the climate niche where humans have thrived for thousands of years.

Chapter Eight
How Do We Feed Ourselves?

"The war against hunger is truly mankind's war of liberation."
—John F. Kennedy

The U.S. is the world's third most agriculturally bountiful country (behind China and India), producing approximately $350 billion a year in agricultural commodities. At that rate of production, we have enough surplus to enable us to export about $177 billion annually in food products worldwide. However, despite growing more than enough food to be self-sufficient, the U.S. imports almost an equal amount—$179 billion in 2021. So, Americans consume only about $171 billion—about half—of our domestically produced food.

There are several reasons for this interesting apparent disparity.

The U.S. has little tropical or subtropical land, but, at present anyway, lots of temperate agricultural acreage suitable for growing grains and livestock. As a result, we have a surplus of grains and meat to sell abroad. On the other hand, we import tropical foods such as bananas as well as fruit and vegetables that are out of season here.

How long, if ever, has it been since you've heard your grocer say about blueberries, for example: "They're out of season?" If you check a blueberry package, you're likely to see "Grown in Mexico."

But the warming will put our domestically grown food products in jeopardy. The examples are many. Consider produce. An estimated 76 percent of our vegetables and fruit are grown in only three states—California, Arizona and Florida.

Here are snapshots of climate-related production problems in these states:

- *California* provides more agricultural products than any other state—most of it from the Central Valley region—accounting for 11 percent of the national total. That output includes more than two-thirds of the nation's fruit and nuts and more than one-third of our vegetables. California's top 10 agricultural commodities among its more than 400 are, in order: dairy products, almonds, grapes, pistachios, cattle, lettuce, strawberries, tomatoes, floriculture and walnuts.

  But, as indicated earlier, the state's verdant Central Valley has a problem with *low temperatures*. Wintertime lows have gotten warmer. This is critical because the valley's perennial crops need off-season dormancy to regenerate. So, temperatures must remain below a certain threshold for at least a minimum amount of time in a growing season, a concept called "chill hours."

  Fruit such as apples, cherries and pears need chill hours of at least 1,000 and were already barely suited to Central Valley conditions 20 years ago. It's projected that more than half of the valley will no longer be suitable for growing crops like apricots, peaches, plums, walnuts and others sometime around the middle of the century.

  In addition, the state's huge Imperial Valley bordering Mexico has almost 500,000 irrigated acres under cultivation. Crops include iceberg lettuce, leaf lettuce, broccoli, cauliflower, cantaloupe, carrots, sweet corn, spinach and watermelon. Most iceberg lettuce consumed in the U.S. is grown here. The climate permits two growing cycles a year, but water will become increasingly problematic. The valley is irrigated by the rapidly shrinking Colorado River.

- *Arizona's* escalating temperatures, in addition to water issues, will substantially reduce the state's output of vegetables and fruit. Arizona is the nation's second-largest producer of lettuce, broccoli, and cantaloupe. Its warm climate allows for year-round vegetable production and earns it recognition as the U.S. winter lettuce capital.

  But a landmark agreement reached in 2022 between the three states that share the lower basin of the Colorado River (Arizona, California, and Nevada) calls for deep cuts in river water allotments through 2026. The cuts aim to prevent the already dangerously low water levels in Lake Mead—the beating heart of the Colorado River delivery system—from dropping further, creating a "dead pool" and disrupting the river's flow. Arizona, with the most junior water rights, is absorbing the bulk of the cuts—21 percent.

  There will be more about severe water shortages in the Southwest in the next chapter.

- *Florida* has a different climate-related problem. Disease.

  In 2017, more than 569,000 acres of citrus groves and 74 million citrus trees could be found in Florida. At that point more than 70 percent of the United States' citrus came from the Sunshine State.

  But, in 2022, 90 percent of the state's groves were infected by a bacterium called *Huanglongbing* (HLB) that originated in China. The pathogen often prevents raw green fruit from ripening, a symptom called "citrus greening." Even when the fruit does ripen, it sometimes falls before it can be picked. Under Florida law, citrus that falls from a tree untouched cannot be sold.

  HLB is spread by yet another invasive species—a tiny insect called the citrus psyllid—that sucks the bacteria into its gut as it feeds on citrus leaves. The insect then infects the next healthy leaf on which it feeds. The pest thrives in temperatures between 60° – 90°F (36°-54°C)—bad news for growers in Florida where temperatures now hover in that range year-round. The bug is there to stay.

Thousands of growers have already quit, leaving "ghost groves" in their wake. More than 7,000 farmers grew citrus in 2004; since then, nearly 5,000 have dropped out. About two-thirds of the factories that processed juice have shut down. The number of packing operations has nose-dived from nearly 80 to 26.

The loss of so many farmers could be the death of the state's second-largest industry (behind tourism) that produced more than 80 percent of the country's orange juice.

Plants aren't the only agricultural commodity adversely affected by high heat. Livestock are also highly susceptible to unfavorable climatic conditions.

Almost all livestock species suffer when temperature and humidity exceed their thresholds of tolerance, resulting in a chain reaction of physiological, behavioral and anatomical alterations that cause reductions in growth, milk yield, meat, eggs, wool and reproductive performance.

Higher temperatures also lead to increases of various diseases as well as a reduction in the availability of livestock feed and fodder.

The U.S. is home to about 90 million beef cattle—about 60 percent of the world total. That's more than a third of a cow per man, woman and child. But, despite the seemingly high number, American's beef consumption has actually declined from 80 pounds per person in 1970 to 57 pounds today.

Vegetarians Have a Point

Food production isn't just being affected by the climate crisis. It's actively contributing to it.

A 2021 study, labeled the "gold standard," claims the global production of food is responsible for a third of all planet-heating gases emitted by human activity, with the use of animals for meat causing twice the pollution of producing plant-based foods.

"The entire system of food production, including the use of farming machinery, spraying of fertilizer and transportation of products, causes 17.3 billion metric tons of greenhouse gases a year," according to the research reported in *The Guardian*.

The raising and culling of animals for food is far worse for the climate than growing and processing fruit and vegetables, confirming previous findings of the outsized impact that meat production, particularly beef, has on the environment.

The use of cows, pigs and other animals for food, as well as producing livestock feed, is responsible for 57 percent of all food production emissions, with 29 percent coming from the cultivation of plant-based foods.... Beef alone accounts for a quarter of emissions produced by raising and growing food. It's estimated that producing one pound of meat generates 35 pounds of GHG.

Since America imports almost as much food as it exports, what's the problem? When the climate begins to affect U.S. agriculture severely, why not simply increase our imports to make up the difference?

The primary reason is that the warming is going to cause dramatic changes in the nature of food importation and exportation worldwide. It's only logical that the U.S., for example, will reduce exporting certain agricultural products that, for climatic reasons, are in short supply in the domestic market. And we will not be alone. Other countries will choose to feed their own populations first rather than export food needed at home.

Mexico—A Case in Point

In recent years, Mexico has dominated the U.S. supply of imported vegetables—providing peppers, cucumbers, tomatoes, corn, pinto beans, broccoli, cabbage, onions, lettuce, celery, squash and spinach. In addition to $6.7 billion worth of vegetables, America also imported $5.3 billion worth of fruit and nuts.

This trade accounted for about 43 percent of total U.S. fruit and vegetable imports from all countries. Tomatoes ($2.3 billion) and avocados ($1.7 billion) are the most popular Mexican vegetable and fruit imports.

In addition, Mexico is one of the larger coffee-producing countries, and the largest producer of organic coffee, accounting for 60 percent of world production. American caffeine lovers consume about $300 million worth of Mexican beans annually.

The U.S. also imports $3.6 billion in wine and beer, $2.7 billion in tequila—along with almost $1 billion in limes and lemons—and $2.2 billion in snack foods.

Worldwide, Mexico is among the leading food producers, ranking first in avocados, lemons and limes; third and fourth for grapefruit and corn; fifth for beans, coconut oil, oranges and poultry; sixth for sugar and ninth for coffee beans.

But the agricultural picture for Mexico will not be rosy for long. Nor will Mexico remain a substantial source of U.S. food imports.

As indicated earlier, according to one study, "Climate change may lead to a 40-70 percent decline in Mexico's current cropland suitability by 2030. Worse, this could soar to an 80-100 percent decline by the end of the century. It's a catastrophe in the making.'

The problem facing our neighbor to the south is that only about 15 percent of its 758,000 square mile land mass is suitable for agriculture. Most of Mexico is arid, semi-arid and mountainous.

In terms of availability of water, Mexico already falls into the "high-stress category," the second-highest level on the list, meaning that it consumes between 40-80 percent of the water available in a year. In some areas, of course, consumption is even higher. Overall, Mexico ranks as the 24th most water-stressed of the 164 nations included in the study.

Many of Mexico's staple crops will increasingly suffer from the warming. Corn, for example, needs a lot of rain or irrigation and doesn't tolerate heat. Coffee bean production will also be affected. Arabica beans are the most common crop. These popular beans need cooler environments to flourish, which is why they thrive in mountainous areas.

Temperature increases associated with the warming will reduce Mexico's viable cropland. Herds and domestic farm animals will also suffer from increasing temperatures and reduced rainfall. Farming will need to move to higher elevations to escape the heat. But, with only about 15 percent of the country viable for agriculture, cooler croplands will be at a premium.

The warming is squeezing Mexico's agriculture in a vice and will greatly reduce Mexico as a source of U.S. food imports.

Does The Warming Benefit Agriculture?

Rep. Lamar Smith (R-TX) claimed in 2014 that climate change "alarmists" ignore the "positive impacts" of more carbon dioxide in the atmosphere, such as increased food production and quality.

This argument has become a staple in propaganda efforts by warming deniers. A second claim is that higher temperatures will increase food production by lengthening growing seasons.

But, according to FactCheck.org, the impact of increased CO_2 levels on agriculture is more complicated than that and may, at best, only have a limited, short-term positive impact.

"Other factors aside, an atmosphere with more CO_2 does boost crop yield in the short term via increased rates of photosynthesis. In the long term, multiple experts told us, the positive effect of increased CO_2 on crops will diminish and the negative impacts of climate change, such as higher temperatures, will grow."

The higher CO_2 levels also encourage the growth of weeds right along with crops. And let's not forget the impact of increasing temperatures on farm workers and livestock.

Smith also claimed that, because of increasing temperatures, "colder areas along the farm belt will experience longer growing seasons."

"This is true," FactCheck countered, "but warmer regions, such as the southern states, will also experience negative effects because of climate change." For example, the northern movement of higher temperatures will temporarily benefit cereal grain production in the upper Great Plains, but, by 2050, these crops may be reduced by 70 percent in lower Great Plains.

FactCheck cited a 2014 UN Intergovernmental Panel on Climate Change (IPCC) report:

> "Latitudinal expansion of cold-climate cropping zones pole wards…may be largely offset by reductions in cropping production in the mid-latitudes as a result of rainfall reduction and temperature increase." The report adds, "For tropical systems where moisture availability or extreme heat rather than frost limits the length of the growing season, there is a likelihood that the length of the growing season and overall suitability for crops will decline."

In other words, these denier claims are scientifically naïve at best or purposely misleading.

In summary, then, the future of food in the coming world of the warming is problematic to say the least. On first blush, it may seem that—because of the complexities of food production and the inexorable march of negative climatic conditions—people may feel powerless to do much about it.

That, however, is not the case.

Before suggesting what can be done, it's probably beneficial to revisit a key point made earlier about *how* we chose to live—the need to lower our expectations and live lives typified by simplicity, self-reliance and sustainability.

If you accept the detailed case just made for the increasing scarcity of food in coming decades—and its substantially higher cost—then the thought exercise that follows should be of interest.

How Are We Going to Feed Ourselves?

Eat less. Without straining to apply any high-level mathematics—something of which I'm frankly not capable—it's easy to calculate that if each American adult (250 million) consumed just the recommended 2,500 calories per day instead of an average of 3,500 (the highest in the world), a net savings of almost 30 percent in caloric consumption would result. That would yield about 30 percent more calories to go around.

The other obvious benefit is a reduction in obesity—a condition that "eats" up about 10 percent of the country's $150 billion annual health budget.

Drastically reduce food waste. The U.S. produces more food waste annually than any other country—approximately 40 million tons. This equates to around 200 pounds of waste per person—a store value of more than $150 billion or $1,500 per family!

Research conducted by the USDA revealed that wasted food in the U.S. makes up around *30 percent of the food supply*.

Why is so much food wasted in America? Some of the main reasons include:

- **Expired/spoiled food**—Food that no longer qualifies as fresh enough to be sold or that is damaged or spoiled and is no longer deemed edible.

- **Damaged or lost during transport**—Food may become exposed to insects or spoiled if transported long distances.

- **Buying more food than one can eat**—This all-too-common practice, of course, can lead to perfectly good food being discarded as waste.

Buy local—While buying food produced close to home may not ensure access to more food, it may be less expensive and fresher than comparable food from the grocery store. Buying local also helps the environment by reducing the distance some foods are transported. Regular visits to local farmers' markets are one means to this end.

Hunting, fishing and foraging—Our ancestors did it! While a trip to the grocery store might be considered a form of foraging, in reality the earth is still a rich source of food if you know where to look and what to look for. Some suggestions include mushrooms, berries, clover, dandelion greens, seaweed, nuts and cattails. There is, of course, copious information on how to prepare foraged items. Hunting and fishing can also be sources of protein.

Grow your own—Although listed last, growing your own food certainly is not the least of the approaches to dealing with food insecurity as the warming unfolds. But there is so much to be said about the subject that it deserves a book all of its own. Luckily there are hundreds of books and websites devoted to all aspects of producing one's own food. So, I'll limit myself to several observations.

> **How much produce can I grow?** The answer, of course, comes down to real estate. How much room do you have for gardening? (If the answer is "none," keep reading.) The consensus among vegetable gardeners is one can expect an average yield of one pound per square foot of space in a well-maintained garden. That applies to all vegetables. One row foot of plants will produce one pound of that vegetable or legume. A row foot is one-linear foot that's one-foot wide. Using pinto beans as an example –115 pounds of pintos provide half the yearly protein requirements for one adult male. That corresponds to approximately 10 by 11.5 feet of garden space.
>
> Still, even under the best of conditions, growing enough for just one or two is tough hoeing.
>
> **Vertical gardening?** Many gardeners turn to growing vegetables vertically, increasing output in a limited space. The best vegetables to grow vertically are beans, peas, tomatoes, cucumbers, melons and squash. There's even an increasingly popular variety of spinach that grows unaided on trellises. Heavy plants like melons and squash usually need additional

support, while tomatoes need to be guided and staked since they don't have tendrils to grab onto surfaces.

Composting—Compost is a mixture of ingredients used as plant fertilizer and to improve soil's physical, chemical and biological properties. It is commonly prepared by decomposing plant and food waste, recycling organic material and manure. Composting will reduce or eliminate the need to buy expensive fertilizers and provide eco-friendly waste disposal.

Alternative spaces? Don't have a backyard? Join a gardener's co-op—a more and more common sight in urban areas. In the country, some farmers are converting parts or all of their acreage into mini-farms to rent. Some offer as much as an acre of land and include water and a small storage shed. In the city, apartment and condo dwellers are turning to roof-top gardens, usually using box containers.

What about fruit? If your yard has sufficient space, a fruit tree or two can be a good investment. It might surprise you, but a good yield for a well-cared for backyard apple tree is about 80-150 apples per season. However, with fertilization, irrigation and appropriate plant protection methods, they can produce from 400 to 800 in a season.

"Easy" source of protein? There's a common saying that "chickens are the gateway livestock." While true, that doesn't mean chickens are particularly easy to raise for protein—eggs or meat. Urban dwellers may face restrictive ordinances if they intend to use their backyards. Chicken feed also doesn't cost "chicken feed." Good feed is expensive. Still, six hens can produce up to 30 eggs a week.

As with gardening, literature on the subject abounds.

What to do with the food you raise. Eat it, obviously. But gardens have a habit of producing mature vegetables within a narrow time frame. Surplus produce can be canned, pickled or flash-frozen for use year-round. And there's also the old-time root cellar. Or, depending on the quantity of surplus, produce can also be bartered.

———————

Although you may not have the pressing need at the moment to engage in any of the food-generating activities just discussed, the time will come—possibly in the next generation—when the impact of the warming on agriculture will demand it. This is why it's important now to consider where and how you choose to live and to begin to adopt and apply some of the lifestyle changes that will become necessary for the survival of future generations.

At the risk of repetition: Surviving the warming will need to be a multi-generational effort.

Chapter Nine
"Whiskey's for Drinkin'; Water's for Fightin'!"*

*This quote is attributed to Mark Twain but lacks authentication. Whether from his pen or not, it accurately describes both the history and future of water.

*"River's ancient face,
Wrinkled with sparkling ripples,
Changing, but changeless"*
—Lorin R. Robinson

Where water is concerned, the warming presents a conundrum. There is, at the same time, too much of it—and too little!

Before we explore this seeming paradox, let's talk about water. What follows is probably more detail than anyone needs to absorb about this important compound. But understanding water is crucial to appreciate how it—both too much and too little—contributes to the dangers posed by the warming.

Approximately 70 percent of the Earth's surface is one great ocean containing about 97.5 percent of its water. Anyone viewing a photo of our planet taken from space—particularly a view of the Pacific—can't help but be amazed by how wet our world is.

Its water also contains a vast quantity of other compounds—salts and minerals—that account for 3.5 percent of its volume. Common table salt (NaCl) makes up 85 percent of these additional ingredients. Anyone who's swallowed a mouthful of seawater can attest to this

Thus, if 97.5 percent of the planet's water is salty and unfit to drink, *only a paltry 2.5 percent remains as freshwater suitable for human consumption.* And, of course, we share that 2.5 percent with all other non-ocean dwelling species.

But how much of this freshwater is readily available for our consumption?

Only about 30 percent of freshwater is accessible for use. The remaining 70 percent is in the form of ice locked in glaciers and ice sheets in places like the Antarctic and Greenland.

Almost all the available freshwater is groundwater that emerges and feeds the streams, rivers, lakes and wetlands. It acts as a reservoir/aquifer that can also be tapped for various uses including agriculture and industry.

Another important source is surface freshwater held in lakes, rivers and reservoirs. But, although critical to the water supply, they contain only about .03 percent of the freshwater.

Overall, this means that—although 2.5 percent of the planet's water is fresh—less than one percent of that total is accessible and available for our use. *Or stated another way, of all the water on Earth, more than 99 percent is unusable by humans.*

It seems unbelievable that freshwater supporting all terrestrial—and freshwater aquatic—life on the planet is so scarce. Is freshwater too scarce or becoming too scarce? Generally, the overall volume of freshwater is said by most to be sufficient to meet human needs at present—except for the fact that the precious commodity is so unevenly distributed around the world.

Right now, according to the World Health Organization (WHO), almost 780 million people live without access to clean water. That's one person in 10. The problem resides primarily in areas such as sub-Saharan Africa where weather patterns simply do not deliver enough rain while other areas may receive a surplus.

But what the future holds is unclear. Save the Water.org predicts that demand for freshwater will increase by 55 percent by 2050.

According to NASA, "Freshwater supplies are being used faster than they are being replaced. Specifically, freshwater levels in aquifers…are decreasing in many locations. The world has major aquifers in places like India, China, France and the United States. Of the 37 aquifers across the world, 21 are getting smaller."

One of these is the Ogallala Aquifer, the largest underground water source in the U.S. It has for decades been pumped at rates thousands of times greater than it's being restored. A Kansas State University study predicts that 69 percent of the aquifer will be drained in the next 50 years at current rates.

This apparent negative water budget is due in part to increasing population—the world population is forecast to reach 10 billion by 2050. Other major factors include the huge and increasing drawdowns for agricultural and industrial applications.

Here are just two examples of extremely high agricultural and industrial water use:

- It takes approximately 1,847 gallons of freshwater to produce one pound of beef—enough water to fill 39 bathtubs all the way to the top. How can that be possible?

  A beef cow eats thousands of pounds of grass, corn, grains and soybeans during its lifetime, and water is necessary to grow this feed. That's one reason why the production of animal products like meat, dairy and eggs requires more water than producing fruit (115 gallons per pound) and vegetables (39 gallons per pound).

- In recent decades, plastic has almost completely replaced glass in the manufacture of bottles. Producing a single plastic bottle takes 17 times as much water as a glass container of similar size. The plastic bottle also requires two times the amount of energy and emits five times as much GHG during its production.

- But fear not. All the plastic we dutifully separate and put on the curb each week is recycled. Wrong. The plastic industry would like us to believe that. But, according to *Consumer Reports*, only about nine percent is recycled. Much of the rest ends up in landfills or in The Great Pacific Garbage Patch—also known as the Pacific Trash Vortex—spanning the ocean from the West Coast to Japan—an estimated 617,000 square miles.

Water Is Unique

Water is the only common substance that can naturally be found in one of the three states of matter—as a solid, liquid or gas. The temperature variation required for water's transformation is quite small. Between 32°F (0°C) and 212°F (100°C), water is liquid. It becomes solid "below freezing" (32° F) or vapor/steam at above 212° F. While water boils at 212° F, it begins to evaporate at 32° F. The process just occurs extremely slowly. As the temperature increases, the rate of evaporation also increases.

Crucial to the delivery of freshwater is *the water cycle* that includes evaporation, condensation, precipitation and infiltration/runoff. The process is global, cyclical and closed in that water is not lost.

Put simply, heat evaporates water from the ocean, lakes, rivers and reservoirs. As it rises, it condenses into vapor droplets and forms clouds. When the droplets are sufficiently cooled at higher altitudes, they fall as rain (hail or snow) and infiltrate groundwater aquifers or are captured in bodies of standing water.

Incidentally, water evaporating from the ocean leaves the salt behind. It's too heavy. It's also important to note that about 90 percent of all evaporated water falls back into the ocean.

Unfortunately, the warming intensifies the water cycle because, as air temperatures increase, water evaporates in higher quantities and more rapidly. Warmer air can hold more water vapor. These factors lead to more intense rainstorms and flooding.

But it doesn't end there. As some areas experience stronger storms, others experience more dry air and drought. In these areas, as temperatures rise, evaporation increases and soil dries out. When rain does come, much of the water can either puddle on the hard ground and evaporate or quickly run off into streams, rivers or lakes. The soil remains dry.

The distribution of rainwater worldwide is very uneven. So, water vapor necessary for the generation of precipitation is problematic.

Drink Up

Water is the body's principal chemical component and makes up about 50-70 percent of body weight. The body depends on water to survive. Every cell, tissue and organ needs water to work properly.

Most people can live only three days without water.

Although recommendations vary somewhat, it is true—as we are constantly told—that the average person can stay properly hydrated with the equivalent of eight glasses of water a day.

"It's not widely known, but water vapor is also Earth's most abundant greenhouse gas. It's responsible for about half of Earth's greenhouse effect—the process that occurs when gases in the atmosphere trap the sun's heat," according to NASA.

"Since the late 1800s, global average surface temperatures have increased by about 2°F (1.1°C). Data from satellites, weather balloons and ground measurements confirm the amount of atmospheric water vapor is increasing as the climate warms—1-2 percent per decade. For every degree Celsius that Earth's atmospheric temperature rises, the amount of water vapor in the atmosphere can increase by about seven percent...."

Obviously, we are in a "Catch 22." The warming encourages more evaporation, increasing the amount of water vapor in the atmosphere but that, in turn, traps more heat and contributes to the global temperature rise.

Before moving on to the warming-generated impact of too much water (i.e., sea level rise), let's briefly consider the story of the Colorado River Basin and the seven states contentiously vying to use its waters. The tale is as old and long and tortuous as the river itself and is emblematic of the almost universal struggle to balance the needs everywhere of economic development and the limited supply of freshwater.

"The Law of the River"

The Colorado River is the lifeblood of the Southwest. Stretching from the 14,000-foot peaks of the Rocky Mountains to the Gulf of California, it travels over 1,400 miles across a watershed that includes seven states, 29 federally recognized tribal reservations and two states in northern Mexico.

Nearly 40 million Americans rely on the river system for drinking water and to support livelihoods ranging from agriculture to manufacturing to recreation. San Diego, Las Vegas, Phoenix and Los Angeles are among the major cities drawing water from its flow.

The watershed is under tremendous pressure—not simply from the demands of increasing food production and growing cities—but also from warming-related extreme weather. This combination has serious implications for the future of agriculture and continued population growth in the region.

Agriculture uses approximately 80 percent of the river's water. It irrigates 15 percent of the nation's farmland and produces 90 percent of our winter vegetables. A recent study found that the largest consumer of river water in the western U.S.—one-half of the total—is irrigation for cattle-feed crops.

For the last 20 years, the river basin has been in a severe drought—thought to be the worst in 1,200 years. May and April, 2021 were the driest on record. Because of high temperatures that increase evaporation and decrease snowpack, the river's flow is expected to drop by 20 percent over the next 30 years. From

2000 to 2015, water consumption exceeded the total river flow three-quarters of the period. In August, 2021 the federal government declared a water shortage in the basin for the first time.

The Hoover Dam was built on the river in 1937 to provide irrigation and hydroelectric power for California and Arizona and to control seasonal flooding, thus aiding the growth of the arid Southwest.

The dam created Lake Mead, the largest reservoir in the country. Its water level, however, has sunk to 27 percent, its lowest since the reservoir was filled for the first time. At that level, the lake is on the verge of becoming a "dead pool" allowing no outflow downstream. Hydroelectric production is also at risk without sufficient water to drive turbines.

With an annual mean discharge of about 15 million acre-feet, the Colorado is not a giant among the world's rivers. But it does traverse one of North America's driest regions, offering opportunities for economic development and growth unmatched by any other water source in this arid landscape.

For the past 100 years these development possibilities have spurred myriad political contests among irrigators, businesses, civic boosters, politicians, tribes, ranchers, government officials, engineers, and, more recently, environmental groups and recreational users—all seeking a voice in river water allocation decisions.

A root cause of these conflicts is the hydrologic reality that, although roughly 90 percent of the river's flow originates in the upper basin states of Colorado, New Mexico, Utah, and Wyoming, much of the demand for the river's water emanates from the more populous and agriculturally active lower basin states of Arizona, California and Nevada.

The many complex legal agreements, compacts and compromises resulting from decades of often contentious litigation have become known generically as "The Law of the River."

The implications for what will, without doubt, be continued reduction in the river's flow are dire.

Chinatown and The Water Knife

The 1974 Roman Polanski film *Chinatown* is more truth than fiction. Set in 1937 Los Angeles, it tells the story of a conspiracy by a cadre of shadowy oligarchs to steal water rights from the Owens Valley, a neighboring farming area. The Oscar-nominated film *noir* starred Jack Nicholson and Faye Dunaway.

Or, if your taste runs to gritty climate fiction, Paolo Bacigalupi's *Water Knife* (2015) takes place in a Southwest of the near future where "water is as valuable as gold." The water supply has been drastically reduced by the warming and control has been taken over by corrupt business magnates. The protagonist is a spy/assassin, known as a "water knife," whose job it is to sabotage the water supply of his employer's competitors.

What can be done to help offset looming freshwater shortages caused by the warming? Solutions are many and varied. Some would require the commitment of effort and resources by government and industry. Others can be undertaken by individuals and families.

- As indicated, agriculture and industry must adopt less water-intensive methods of production. Obviously, it would also be helpful if consumers would reduce their demand for water-hungry animal products.

- Energy production is the second largest consumer of water resources globally after agriculture. Thermoelectric power plants in the United States withdraw as much freshwater as farms. Continued migration to non-fossil fuel energy sources will help free up a portion of this water in addition to reducing CO_2 levels in the atmosphere.

- Infrastructure needs upgrading. It is estimated that 2.1 trillion gallons of treated water in the U.S. is lost each year from leaking pipes.

- The lack of adequate water treatment is resulting in widespread pollution of freshwater resources. One report estimates that two billion tons of human, animal and industrial waste are dumped untreated into freshwater bodies each year.

- Despite their high cost, desalination plants should be considered for water-scarce regions near enough to the ocean to make them feasible. Two plants in Perth, Australia, for example, provide 45 percent of the water for a city of two million.

- Rainwater harvesting is being practiced in cities around the world—both by residents and the cities themselves—to capture millions of gallons of freshwater from roofs and other surfaces. Regulations in most places forbid drinking the runoff, earmarking it instead for watering lawns and gardens, replacing potable water.

- Those homeowners with septic systems can divert the "gray" water from tubs, showers and sinks to a holding tank to reuse for watering or cleaning purposes. Gardeners should try to restrict decorative vegetation to that which is drought resistant.

- It may be hard to believe, but a dishwasher is apparently a greener choice than hand washing your dishes—if it's a newer model washing a full load. This may seem impossible since dishwashers are constantly spraying water, but newer ones use less water than hand washing. Getting dishes clean in the sink can use up to 27 gallons of water per load. The claim is that an Energy Star certified dishwasher can use as little as three gallons per load.

- Reduced water-flow devices for showers and toilets are significant water savers.

The other half of the water story concerns *too much*—the ever-rising ocean fed by an estimated 425 billion tons of freshwater annually flowing from melting glaciers, ice caps and ice sheets. Using 1900 as a benchmark, SLR has been over one foot to date. Predictions are that it will be at or near three feet by 2050.

At three feet, how much *terra firma* will the U.S. lose? According to *Climate Central*, the figure is an astonishing 29,000 square miles—home to approximately 123 million people. If you are someone who prefers visualization, insert Sea Level Rise and Coastal Flooding Impacts in your browser to see maps and animations showing how much land the ocean will gobble up at SLRs of 1-10 feet.

As discussed in detail earlier, SLR is only part of the problem. The increasing number and severity of tropical storms and hurricanes, particularly along our Atlantic and Gulf shores, will continue to meet out damage and destruction from high winds, torrential rains and flooding that will often stretch hundreds of miles inland from original point of contact.

Add ingredients such as increasing temperatures and humidity to the violent weather and one has a stew that's pretty indigestible. Migration—sooner better than later—will be the only answer for those who are able.

It would be nice to end the chapter on a positive note. I wish I were able to do so.

Let's talk about global warming's "Evil Twin."

It's difficult to believe that humans could screw up a body of water that contains an estimated 343 million trillion (343 quintillion gallons) of H_2O. But one should never underestimate our ingenuity.

It's been found that about 30 percent of the CO_2 in the atmosphere dissolves in the ocean. That might seem like a good thing—the ocean acting like a huge carbon sink taking CO_2 out of the air. But it seems that nothing comes without a price. Water and carbon dioxide combine to form carbonic acid (H_2CO_3). The ocean's average pH (a measure of acidity) is now around 8.1 (which is alkaline).

But as the ocean continues to absorb more CO_2, the pH decreases, and the ocean becomes more acidic.

Marine scientists are calling ocean acidification the warming's "Evil Twin." It's estimated at the current rate of increase, the ocean will be *150 times more acidic* than it is today by the end of the century. The impact on marine life is difficult to predict, but many species simply will not have the time or ability to adapt to the more acidic conditions.

Ocean acidification is already affecting many marine animals—organisms, for example, like shellfish and corals that make hard shells and skeletons. As acidification increases, these organisms will have difficulty building and maintaining their shells, skeletons and other structures. If the pH gets too low, shells and skeletons can even begin to dissolve.

So human generated CO_2 isn't the only negatively affecting terrestrial agriculture, causing drought and desertification, it is also reducing the ocean's ability to serve as an alternative source of food.

CHAPTER TEN
Keeping the Lights On

"Be Careful What You Wish For!" —Unknown

The history of *homo sapiens* can be written from many perspectives. One point of view might be our unrelenting quest—and insatiable need—for energy.

Our ancient ancestors had only one source of energy—their bodies. They could run, lift, climb and throw—but only as fast, as high, and as far as their muscles permitted. This put them at a grave disadvantage because they were more often prey than predator.

Then came fire. It is, of course, not accurate to say humans discovered fire. Volcanoes and wildfires were all around them. It is not known for certain when fire was first controlled by our ancestors, but evidence for their use of fire by about 400,000 years ago has wide scholarly support.

Fire was a start. It enabled early humans to warm themselves, light up the very long and dark nights, frighten off predators and cook food to make it more palatable and easier to digest.

The first truly modern application of fire didn't occur until about 3000 BC when it was used to smelt metals to fabricate tools and weapons. Prior to that, soft metals like copper and gold were beaten into shape—ending the Stone Age at about 6000 BC.

In the same timeframe, people realized they could harness the wind. The earliest record of a ship under sail appears on an

Egyptian vase from about 3500 BC. And the wheel is also thought to have been invented around that time, allowing the application of animal power to transportation. Spoked wheels were crafted in about 2000 BC, which considerably reduced their weight.

The Chinese, around 4000 BC, discovered a rock that would burn. Coal initially had limited uses in both the East and West—home heating and smelting—until the invention of the first steam engine in 1712. It changed the world forever. The steam engine made big factories possible and was used to power trains and ships—even some early automobiles like the Stanley Steamer.

The demand for coal skyrocketed, marking the advent of the Industrial Revolution.

Oil was first discovered by the Chinese in 600 BC, but its discovery in Pennsylvania in 1859 and in Texas in 1901 set the stage for the new oil economy. Petroleum was much more adaptable and flexible than coal.

Gasoline was a byproduct of refining crude oil to make kerosene for lighting. There was no use for gasoline at the time, but, in the early 1890s, automobile inventors realized that gasoline had value as a motor fuel. In 1911, gasoline outsold kerosene for the first time. And, by 1920, there were about nine million gasoline-powered vehicles in the United States.

Today there are about 300 million.

Another milestone in the human quest for energy was the discovery of electricity. The phenomenon was understood by many early scientists, but Benjamin Franklin is given the credit. In 1752, Franklin conducted his iconic experiment using a kite and key on a stormy day.

Commercial production of electricity, however, didn't begin until 1873 with the coupling of a dynamo to a hydraulic turbine. The mechanical production of electric power began the Second Industrial Revolution and made possible several significant early inventions using electricity.

So why the history lesson? It allows me to point out the irony of our situation.

Our millennia-long quest for energy has allowed us to build a civilization unimaginable to our ancestors. But it has also led us to the brink of what has been called "The Sixth Extinction." Satisfying our hunger for energy will, over the next century, cause the extinction of many species—possibly our own.

As some wise individual once said: "Be careful what you wish for."

That human-caused emissions of CO_2 and other greenhouse gases since the Industrial Revolution are responsible for the warming is indisputable.

"Data for the past 2,000 years show that the atmospheric concentrations of CO_2, CH_4, and N_2O—three important long-lived greenhouse gases—have increased substantially since about 1750. Rates of increase in levels of these gases are dramatic. CO_2, for instance, never increased more than 30 ppm during any previous 1,000-year period but has already risen 30 ppm in the past two decades.

"These increases in greenhouse gas concentrations… are largely attributable to human activities since the Industrial Revolution (1800)," according to the American Chemical Society.

To say it didn't have to be this way is probably disingenuous. It's not as if we weren't warned. Some scientists in the nineteenth century noted the potential for the then newly named greenhouse gases to warm the Earth. Newspaper accounts in the early twentieth century pointed to climatic changes taking place that could be attributed to carbon emissions.

But, by then, the proverbial die had been cast. Industry, utilities and car makers were committed to coal and petrochemicals. And the public? What did we know? Our homes had lights, heat, and cooling. We were able to "See the USA in our Chevrolet." Life was good, particularly after WWII, and for the first time in human history, energy was plentiful—and cheap.

It is interesting to note that all the new energy sources developed in the past 140 years have used non-fossil fuels. As a precursor to non-carbon generated energy, the world's first hydroelectric power plant began operation on the Fox River in Appleton, Wisconsin in 1882.

In the century to come, other clean sources of energy would debut—the first nuclear power plant went online in 1951, solar panels for electric generation were demonstrated in 1954 and the first wind generator "farm" began providing power in 1975.

Yet, despite the desperate need to kick the fossil-fuel habit and convert to clean energy, today (2024) less than 30 percent of the world's energy needs are being met with these six relatively old technologies.

So, What About Carbon Capture or Hydrogen Energy?

Carbon capture isn't new. It's been practiced since 1972. It also isn't a complex method of curbing greenhouse gas emissions. CO_2 is captured at the point of emission and transported to an underground storage space where, over a long period of time, the carbon will calcify and become solid.

ExxonMobil claims to be a global leader in carbon capture with more than 1,500 miles of CO_2 pipeline—the largest network in the U.S.—and access to 15 onshore sites for storage. The company claims it has the potential to reduce emissions by more than 100 million tons a year.

Sounds good, until you remember that we are currently dumping *37 billion* tons of CO_2 into the atmosphere. And, of course, the carbon capturers are only taking low hanging fruit. There's no way, for example, to capture the carbon coming out of a car's tailpipe.

Hydrogen has also been getting a lot of attention recently as an alternative to carbon-based fuels for vehicles. But there are some practical issues in implementation. One is the need to build an extensive network of hydrogen fuel stations. Also, hydrogen is extremely explosive and dangerous to transport and handle (remember the Hindenburg?) and needs expensive, strong tanks to be stored either in gas or liquid form.

The "why" we've lagged in adoption of carbon-less technologies was dealt with extensively in an earlier chapter. But, at the risk of repetition, one major reason lies at the doorsteps of the petrochemical, coal, utility and automotive industries. Despite knowing better, they spent untold millions over several decades on disinformation, lobbying, and pseudoscience designed to convince the public that they were not responsible for the warming, or, failing that, to downplay its consequences.

Nuclear Phobia

The consensus is that nuclear power generation could have been a significant contributor to replacing fossil fuels. Unfortunately, three frightening nuclear accidents substantially retarded its development.

These incidents, however, were not the fault of the technology. A combination of poor design and poorly trained operators led to the failures at Three-Mile Island (1979), Chernobyl (1986) and Fukushima (2011).

Today there are 440 nuclear plants around the world producing a mere 10 percent of its electrical power. At 19 percent, the U.S. is ahead of the curve, but only two new plants are currently under construction. Meanwhile, many existing American plants are old and being decommissioned. Worldwide the number of plants under construction is 55.

Thus, the U.S. is not likely to increase its share of nuclear-generated power in years to come. Obviously, the residual fear left by the three disasters is partly to blame—as is the self-serving anti-nuclear stance of the petrochemical and coal industries.

A snapshot of the U.S energy infrastructure reveals an enormous spider web—the largest in the world—stretching to every corner, nook and cranny of the country. It consists of 200,000 miles of high-tension lines and 5.5 million miles of secondary distribution lines. Pipelines for distribution of petrochemical products total 2.5 million miles.

Considering the strong potential for climatic disruption of these two energy grids by the warming, one needs to ask about their robustness—particularly considering recent performance issues in Texas. And the shutting down of a major pipeline on the East Coast by Russian hackers also raises the question of their security.

The State that Couldn't Keep the Lights On

The contiguous U.S. electrical power grid is separated into three parts. Two make up the Eastern Interconnection and the Western Interconnection and power 47 of the lower 48 states. The third grid—with the ironic name of the Electric Reliability Council of Texas (ERCOT)—is separate from the other two.

Not included are El Paso and parts of northeast and southeast Texas. ERCOT powers about 90 percent of Texas residents.

Not coincidentally, Texas—the second largest state in the U.S. with the second highest population—claims to be *the energy capital of the world*, hosting the headquarters of more than 500 oil and gas exploration and production companies and hundreds of firms providing supporting activities. The state also has nine refineries handling 2.3 million barrels of crude oil every day, making it one of largest oil producers in the world. It is reputed to have the ninth largest economy globally.

In 1935, President Roosevelt signed the Federal Power Act, which gave the government authority to regulate interstate power lines. The Lone Star State, which frequently insists on marching to a different drummer, decided it wanted no part of the act. ERCOT was formed in 1970.

In February 2021, the state was hit by a massive storm with frigid temperatures resulting in a power grid crisis during which all sources of electricity were challenged. The inability of power plants to perform in the extreme cold was the number one cause of a statewide outage, leaving an unprecedented 11 million Texans freezing and in the dark for as long as three days, and resulting in as many as 700 deaths.

Unlike most other states that safely endured the storm, "Texas had stubbornly declined to require winterization of its power plants and, just as critically, its natural gas facilities. In large part, that's because the state's politicians and the regulators they appoint are often captive to the oil and gas industry, which lavishes them with millions of dollars a year in campaign contributions. During the February freeze, the gas industry failed to deliver critically needed fuel, and, while Texans of all stripes suffered, the industry scored windfall profits of about $11 billion—creating debts that residents and businesses will pay for at least the next decade," reported *Texas Monthly*.

In July 2022, ERCOT faced another crisis—a blistering statewide heat wave that led to a call for Texans voluntarily to reduce demand on a couple of especially hot afternoons when it looked as if all those air conditioners might overwhelm generating capacity.

This led Slate.com to question if, as ERCOT had claimed, its grid is "fixed."

But receiving one's power from one of the other two national grids is no guarantee that you'll be safe from serious outages. While Texas took the number one spot for outages in 2021, Louisiana and California were numbers two and three. In many years, California ranks first.

The Energy Information Administration reports that the average person in the U.S. spent over eight hours without power in 2020—the worst year for outages in records going back to 2013.

"Power outages have been on the rise for more than a decade." At this point, the United States "experiences more electric outages than any other developed nation," according to a report from the Pew Charitable Trusts.

Outages overall cost $18-33 billion a year, depending on who's counting and what's included. A report by the U.S. Department of Energy cites weather-related damage as the leading cause.

The report and the Pew research both acknowledge that an aging infrastructure is also part of the problem. Some of the power grid dates to the earliest onset of electricity. Replacement or substantial upgrading could not only make them better prepared to withstand severe weather, but also be better protected against cyberattack.

The nation's energy system earned a C– in 2021 from the American Society of Civil Engineers. Proper upgrading of the power grid is estimated to *cost in the trillions of dollars.*

It may appear that some progress could be made. President Biden's $1 trillion infrastructure package allocates $550 billion for various infrastructure programs over five years, but only *$65 billion* is to rebuild the electric grid. It calls for thousands of miles of new power lines and expanding renewable energy.

For comparison purposes, cleaning up after Hurricane Ida in August 2021 cost an estimated $100 billion. How much of that was devoted to repairs to the electrical grid and pipelines is difficult to parse. But the storm stretched all the way from Louisiana to New York where flooding led to the closing of the subway system—at a cost of $18 billion.

Biden's bill followed years of failed efforts in Washington to overhaul physical infrastructure, improvements that advocates have said will boost the economy and create jobs. The last major infrastructure bill, costing $305 billion over five years, was approved in 2015 but limited to expenditures on transportation.

The Cyber Punching Bag

New York Times veteran cyber reporter Nicole Perlroth in her book *This Is How They Tell Me the World Will End* (2021) retells the tale of Russia's 2017 devastating cyberattacks on the Ukraine after getting ahold of NSA's best hacking tools.

You'll have to read the book to see for yourself if the hyperbolic title is supported by the tale it tells. I did. It does.

By 2019, the tally of damages from that single Russian attack had exceeded $10B.

Clearly Russia has been using Ukraine as a proving ground for developing and perfecting its cyberweapons. Perlroth said Ukrainians repeatedly warned her: "You're next."

But the Russian hackers are already here and have been for some time—as are those of other U.S. adversaries including North Korea, Iran and China.

The public generally first became aware of Russian hacking activities during the 2016 presidential campaign when its efforts were directed at helping Donald Trump's election bid.

And the U.S. power grid is also a major target.

Security firm Symantec warns that a series of recent hacker attacks not only compromised energy companies in the U.S. and Europe but also resulted in the intruders gaining hands-on access to power grid operations—enough control that they could induce blackouts on American soil at will.

Never had hackers been shown to have that level of control of American power systems. The only comparable situations, Symantec stressed, had been the repeated hacker attacks on the Ukrainian grid that caused the power outages in 2015 and 2016—the first known hacker-induced blackouts, as Perlroth explained.

A recent government report describes a massive Russian hacking campaign to infiltrate America's "critical infrastructure"—things like power plants, nuclear generators and water facilities. The joint report from the FBI and Department of Homeland Security claims that Russian hackers gained access to computers across the targeted industries and collected sensitive data including passwords, logins, and information about energy generation. While the report doesn't specify any identifiable sabotage, the intrusion could set up future attacks that do more than just record data.

At the outset of the war in Ukraine, the Biden administration warned of the potential for Russian cyberattacks on American soil, and, in newly unsealed indictments, the Justice Department has released details about cyberattacks it says Russians have launched in the past.

"The Russians pose a serious and persistent threat," Deputy Attorney General Lisa Monaco told *60 Minutes*. "It is very much the type of activity that we are warning about today when it comes to Russia's response to the world's response to the horror in Ukraine."

Between 2012 and 2017, the Justice Department says three Russian intelligence agents and accomplices targeted the energy sector, hacking hundreds of companies and organizations around the world. Russian hackers also managed to get inside the computer network at a nuclear power company in Kansas, the indictment says.

Monaco said that although these incidents occurred in the past, Americans should be prepared for similar attacks. "We are seeing Russian state actors scanning, probing, looking for opportunities, looking for weaknesses in our systems on critical infrastructure, on businesses," Monaco said.

The other important component in our energy infrastructure is the 2.5-million-mile network of pipelines delivering natural gas and other oil products around the country. These are also targeted by hackers.

The most recent incident to gain national attention involved a ransomware attack by Russians on the Colonial pipeline, the largest pipeline system for refined oil products in the U.S. It's 5,500 miles long and can carry three million barrels of fuel per day between Texas and New York.

The May 2021 hack forced Colonial to halt operations. The company said the ransomware attack targeted its information technology systems and that the pipeline did not appear to suffer any damage.

Colonial restarted its operations six days later. The shutdown sparked panic-buying and hoarding that overwhelmed gas stations in the Southeast. A significant percentage of gas stations in Virginia, Georgia, North Carolina and South Carolina were without fuel.

Cybersecurity experts have been warning for years about the threat posed by ransomware attacks on U.S. infrastructure in the wake of thousands of successful hacks of computer systems operated by governments, school districts, companies and hospitals. Combatting attacks requires that governments and businesses beef up their defenses in order to block intrusions and that diplomatic pressure be put on countries harboring cybercriminals.

Sadly, it appears not enough is being done on either front. The private sector, in particular, is lagging behind in hardening its computer systems because of the expense. Companies apparently find it less expensive simply to pay the ransom and pass those costs on to consumers.

Colonial was reluctant to divulge the size of its ransom, but, according to numerous sources, the company paid the Russians $5 million to return control.

Colonial also made headlines in 2017 when it shut down significant portions of its pipelines during Hurricane Harvey. During that period, gasoline and diesel prices rose to multi-year highs—just another example of how severe weather affects energy infrastructure.

———

What are we to make of all of this? What will be the future of energy in our increasingly warming and geopolitically unstable world?

Three things seem abundantly clear:

- Much of our energy distribution system—particularly the power grids—needs significant upgrading to the tune of trillions of dollars.

- Not only do the systems need drastic improvement, but they also need hardening to resist the ever more severe weather the warming will inflict—increasing temperatures and wild temperature fluctuations, hurricanes, flooding, increased tornadic activity and wildfires. It will also need hardening to resist cyber predation.

- Much of the cost of making necessary improvements will be passed along to consumers—adding to the inevitability of serious inflation.

Chapter Eleven
Get Thee Off The Grid!

"For eons humankind has sought easy accessibility to large qualities of inexpensive energy. So now what?"
—Lorin R. Robinson

In preparing to survive the warming, what then are we and succeeding generations supposed to do to ensure we have the affordable and dependable energy resources needed to live our lives?

My answer comes in five short words: Get thee off the grid!

Easier said than done, you say. And you're absolutely correct. But—thinking long-term as we are—this is probably the only recourse.

Whether or when you or your family now or in the next generations strive to become energy independent, of course, depends on your situation or what you intend it to be. For example:

- Do you own a single-family residence? Obviously, converting to solar is usually not a viable option if you live in an apartment, condo or most townhomes—unless the structures as a whole convert.

- Are there zoning issues that will preclude you from using solar panels?

- Do you plan to relocate to a more desirable part of the country to try to avoid as much as possible of the worst the warming will bring? Or recommend that members of your family relocate?

- If relocation is part of the plan, a major consideration should be the suitability of the new residence for going off-grid. Many homeowners may have the means to install slightly larger capacity systems than they need. The excess power can be sold to the electrical service provider and help reduce systems costs.

- Obviously, if building a new residence is a possibility, solar electricity and solar hot water should be considered.

This book, of course, is not a technical or how-to-do-it manual. If or when you or family members think seriously about alternative energy, it's best to consult a local solar-power professional. The residential solar landscape is changing rapidly as panels and distribution systems are improved and as the government fiddles with tax credits available for conversion. But here are some things to consider:

- The 2022 Inflation Reduction Act includes thousands of dollars in tax credits and rebates for consumers who install solar panels or make other energy-efficient upgrades to their homes.

- The Residential Clean Energy Credit (25D) offers a 30 percent tax credit for a rooftop solar project.

- The cost of solar energy has dropped significantly in recent years. A decade ago, a 6kw-hour residential solar system could cost more than $50,000. Now, the total cost of a typical home installation ranges from $15,000 to $20,000.

- A 6kw system is sufficient to power a small-demand energy household. The federal tax rebate would reduce the cost to $11,500-$14,000.

- But don't forget that the annual savings from not buying electricity would help pay for the system—in as few as five years, depending on system cost and the size of your monthly bill. Also, as indicated, any excess power can sometimes be sold to the electrical service provider and help defray system costs.

- For something less elaborate, solar-powered generators are on the market. They're not meant for whole home use but can provide up to 2000 watts of emergency power. And they come equipped with solar panels.

Just parenthetically, what's wrong with using wind for generating residential power? The list of "why nots" is rather long but comes down to this. According to Alex Wilson writing in *Green Building Advisor*:

"Home-scale wind power rarely makes good economic sense—except in locations where there is strong, steady wind. I'm disappointed by this. I would really like to think that I could install a cost-effective wind turbine at my home, but I can't. A good site for wind power—where there is a strong 15 mph wind much of the time—wouldn't be a place you'd want to live."

And what about cooling? Obviously, if you convert to solar energy, you're not going to want to strain system capacity running a traditional air conditioning system. The two answers are low-tech but effective— "swamp" or evaporative coolers and attic fans.

Swamp coolers work by pulling in warm air that is then cooled by passing it through a continuously moistened pad. The moisture in the pad evaporates, which results in cooler and more humid air being pumped into the home. That being said, evaporative coolers work best in dry climates.

The process is completely natural and evaporative coolers are more efficient than traditional ACs. They use about 10 times less energy and typically cost less upfront.

And here's an oldie but goodie—the attic fan in two varieties.

As outside temperatures rise, so does the temperature inside the attic, acting like a giant heating blanket over your entire home. Attic temperatures can run as high as 160° F. An attic fan can help reduce this effect by exhausting that stale, hot air outside, lowering the temperature of your attic and the rest of the home. Although attic fans won't be as effective as a dedicated AC, they're more affordable and usually require less extensive installation.

The other option is the whole-house attic fan. Despite their relatively simple operation, they can have a big impact on the overall temperature of your home. Whole-house fans all work in essentially the same way: by pulling cooler night air into your home through open doors and windows, pushing that air into your attic, and exhausting the hot attic air outside through vents in the roof. This lowers the temperature by creating a breeze throughout your home, as well as cooling the warm air in the attic.

Keeping warm in winter, however, could be more of a challenge.

In 2022, an estimated 48 percent of homes in the U.S. were heated with natural gas, 37 percent with electricity. Propane use is at about 10 percent.

Natural gas today is the least expensive alternative. But supply and distribution problems in the long-term—as with electricity—may result in dependability issues, shortages and higher prices.

Most electrically heated homes use baseboard, space heaters or radiant heat in the floors that are relatively expensive to operate. These would seem to work well with a solar system, but to handle the load, its capacity would have to be increased significantly over that required to meet basic power needs.

Is the Heat Pump an Answer?

Without doing a deep dive into heating technologies, there's a potentially useful new approach—*the solar-powered heat pump.*

An air-source heat pump uses advanced technology and the refrigeration cycle to heat or cool a home. A heat pump can heat, but it can also cool. The pump can switch from heat mode to air condition mode by reversing to the refrigeration cycle, providing cooling and a reduction in humidity.

As one manufacture waxes enthusiastically:

"No need for pumps, tanks, glycol, water lines, controllers, drain-back systems, or plumbing issues that you find with other solar heating systems. This high-efficiency solar heater is a heat pump that provides 12,000 BTU of heat per hour, for pennies a day! And unlike typical solar space heating solutions…there is no wasted investment in the summer—this unit is also a high-efficiency solar air conditioner!"

The manufacturer cautions, however, that the unit is not "strictly off the grid." During the day it operates primarily on solar power but may use small amounts of electricity from the utility if needed.

Other less techy solutions include forced-air wood burning furnaces and fireplaces with heatilators.

Wood-burning furnaces can be used indoors or outdoors. They use blowers, existing ductwork and heat exchangers to distribute the heat.

Fireplace heatilators provide efficient distribution of heat usually only within the room where located. But, teamed with an effective ceiling fan, multiple rooms can benefit. Fireplaces may be either wood or gas burning.

Finally, the simplest and most cost-effective "technology" of all—the sun. A home with many south-facing windows and tile flooring can capture a great deal of heat from old Sol during the day—so much, in fact, that many solar-designed homes need to use awnings or blinds to control the heat. Teamed with strategically placed fans, this solar heat can help warm a significant portion of a home—particularly if it has an open floor plan.

And let us not forget hot water. Solar hot water systems are relatively simple and require very little power. They consist of black pipes arrayed on a roof through which water is pumped and heated by the sun. The water feeds into the hot side of the home's water system. An electric hot water heater may be added to the system as backup.

People who like their homes toasty warm in winter and artic cold in summer are not going to be completely happy with any of these heating and cooling suggestions. Nor will folks who like semi-scalding showers.

But remember that surviving the warming will require a lowering of expectations. To repeat our mantra: simplicity, self-reliance and sustainability.

Earthship Anyone?

Along Highway 64, just a few miles from Taos in northern New Mexico, homes rise from the dusty high-mesa with futuristic, phantasmagorical shapes resembling large scale versions of Hobbit houses. They are known as earthships—completely self-contained off-the-grid homes.

They are made mostly from recycled materials—what some might call trash—like used tires tightly packed with dirt for insulation. Recycled bottles and cans are also often used structurally as part of exterior walls that are then plastered with adobe. Sometimes the bottle ends are left exposed to create colorful designs lighted from within. The thick walls provide excellent insulation against extremes of desert heat and cold.

There are no power, water or sewage lines. Electricity is generated by solar panels. Water is harvested from rain and snow melt and collected in cisterns within the homes. "Grey" water from sinks and showers is collected and recycled for use in watering gardens.

Like sunflowers, the homes are all oriented to the south-tracking sun. They have long expanses of floor-to-ceiling windows that transmit sunshine—an average of 300 days a year in Taos—to tile floors, providing the home's heat. Excess heat is controlled by awnings and shades.

Architect Michael Reynolds is the father of the earthship concept, building his first one in 1972 and teaching others ever since. His invented profession—Biotecture—aims to bring people and the planet together through his earthships.

According to Reynolds, earthships address all six major needs that people have for survival—comfortable shelter, water, electricity, treating sewage, handling garbage and producing food. His firm, Earthship Biotecture, has created more than 1,000 highly energy-efficient structures to date in 40 countries, used for everything from luxury rentals to disaster-relief shelters.

"Your typical human still lives for the American dream," Reynolds said. "You know, my custom home with a dressing room that has room for 60 pairs of shoes.... Those days, in my mind, are already gone."

Reynolds cites skyrocketing energy prices and a growing desire to live sustainably amid climate change as fueling demand for homes that, like these, are generally self-contained.

Chapter Twelve
Employment Opportunities

"There are no jobs on a dead planet!"
—Sign held by a protester

"PRC ENVIRONMENTAL

DEMOLITION SERVICES

We Build Vacant lots"!

—Sign on a cleared lot in Biloxi, MS after Katrina (2005)

It is said that some people work to live while others live to work. There are no statistics indicating how many among us belong in one category or the other. But I think it's safe to assume that most Americans do not view their jobs as ends in themselves but as means to an end—paying the bills.

I did have one friend, however, who took a different spin on working. He made good money dealing blackjack at Las Vegas casinos. When he'd saved enough money— "fun tickets" as he called them—he'd quit his job and travel the world until his tickets ran out. Then he'd head back to the tables and start all over again.

Few of us have the luxury of leading his hedonistic lifestyle. Unless you're retired and have a good retirement income or were fortunate enough to be born "into" money, work—a career—is necessary. Of course, it would help to love what you do. But, unfortunately, not everyone can be that lucky.

Love or Hate Relationship?

Gallup's recent annual Work and Education Poll found that about three in five (60 percent) employed adults in the United States like their jobs; but only a fortunate one-third of workers love their occupations.

Unfortunately, as with virtually everything else in the coming world of the warming, the world of work will be turned topsy-turvy. But, to date, few have begun to think about its impact on how we'll make a living in the face of its onslaught.

Future employment prospects are one of the least studied of all the effects of the warming. Most consideration is being given to improving short-term prospects for those jobs related to the mitigation (reducing) of the warming's impact. Among the top-ranking positions listed by Yale University's Climate Connections:

- Wind turbine service technicians
- Hydrologists
- Solar photovoltaic installers
- Atmospheric and space scientists
- Soil and plant scientists
- Conservation scientists
- Environmental science and protection technicians
- Environmental engineers

"Demand for wind turbine service technicians will grow faster than any U.S. occupation between now and 2029 (58%), according to the Bureau of Labor Statistics. Similarly, despite a slowdown in 2020, solar photovoltaic installers can expect strong job prospects. It's the third-fastest growing job category (47%)."

So, if you're college-bound, have a technical or scientific bent, and are looking for a major that could lead to a secure career, this list could be of value. Unfortunately, those already in the work force would need to obtain an appropriate college degree to qualify for most of these positions. The exceptions would be wind and solar power technicians for whom training could probably be available.

But what will be the longer-term impact of the warming on the many thousands of other jobs listed within the 22 employment segments catalogued by the Bureau of Labor Statistics—the ones held by most of the rest of us?

Here we go again with more "thought exercises."

This Ain't Chicken Feed

I don't know about you, but I occasionally skim lists of things that interest me. So, I randomly scanned the Agricultural job segment in the Bureau of Labor statistics. One job popped up. "Chicken Sexer." I just had to look it up:

"A chicken sexer distinguishes the sex of chicks and other hatchlings. Chicken sexers have a very important role in mass poultry production. Hundreds of thousands of chicks are born daily, and producers need to know the sex of those chicks so as to know what role they will have in the industry. This skill is pivotal to the sector's industrial growth. Today, chicken sexers can start at $60,000 a year, close to double what other workers make in a hatchery."

This could be a very secure position as the warming unfolds. No matter how bad things become, I suspect chickens will always be with us.

"Climate change is now widely acknowledged as one of the great—if not the greatest—challenge facing humanity in the coming decades.... (I)t will endanger the livelihood of hundreds of millions and impose increasing costs on our societies.... Indeed, the economic impact has been estimated at something between five and 20 percent of global GDP by 2050, a colossal burden," according to the International Labour Organization.

As suggested earlier, when it comes to the warming, many people see the world in rose-colored glasses tinted by all the incessant talk about ways "we" are going to save the planet.

President Biden's heart is in the right place, but he's misleading the public with claims that the United States will achieve a 50-52 percent reduction from 2005 levels in net greenhouse gas pollution by 2030— "building on progress to date and by positioning American workers and industry to tackle the climate crisis."

Many believe that goal is unrealistic—no matter how many electric U.S. Post Office vehicles he puts on the road. In any case there's the possibility that Biden will not be sitting in the White House in 2025 and Donald Trump or a clone may giddily dismantle his CO_2 reduction plans as Trump did with President Obama's.

And this bears repeating. To date less than 30 percent of the world's energy is provided by non-fossil fuels. Meanwhile CO_2 ppm has reached a record 425 while the world continues to dump 37 billion tons of that greenhouse gas into the atmosphere each year.

Let us also not forget that the U.S. is the second highest CO_2 contributor globally. China is first, contributing over 10 million tons annually.

What are China's plans? "We aim to have CO_2 emissions peak before 2030 and achieve carbon neutrality before 2060," according to President Xi Jinping. At the speed with which the warming is unfolding, Xi's 2060 commitment is the very definition of "too little, too late."

And, despite good-faith efforts to reign in greenhouse gasses, there still looms the massive and uncontrollable outgassing of billions of tons of CO_2 and methane as the Arctic and Siberian tundra melt.

It is difficult, of course, to predict with any certainty how the warming will affect the ways in which people make a living. And the further into the future such forecasting goes, the less reliable it will be considering all the unforeseen variables that will arise. But from what we now know it is possible to make educated guesses about some jobs and professions within those 22 employment segments.

Let's look first at one of the earliest of the segments to be hit by the warming.

Real Estate

Folks involved in selling and buying real estate—both residential and commercial—are facing a rocky road. As discussed in an earlier chapter about migration, soon many residents of sea-side counties and the Deep South and Southwest will realize it's time to relocate in order to escape the ever-rising water, heat and humidity.

Let's revisit Florida's Miami-Dade County, for example. It's estimated that $5.7 billion in residential property is at risk of being flooded by 2050 in just Miami Beach alone. Across all of Miami-Dade County, it's closer to $8.7 billion. Miami-Dade contains 26 percent of all U.S. homes at risk from rising seas, according to Zillow, an online real estate company. And then there's the additional impact on many billions of dollars' worth of commercial buildings in the county.

Obviously much of the Florida real estate market will drown in the rising waters. Remember that the peninsula may become an archipelago by 2050 as the waters rise. And, as the market shrinks, so do opportunities for realtors. The same will be true in most seaside cities.

Oddly, however, realtors in other parts of the country will benefit from the exodus from the coasts and increasingly sweltering southern landscapes. The immigrants will need housing elsewhere, so, temporarily at least, realtors in Minnesota—as an example—may be quite busy. That's, of course, until available housing runs out.

In migrant-targeted areas, however, savvy entrepreneurs will build additional housing to accommodate the immigrants—at least those who come with the necessary financial resources. Some of the new construction will have to be low-income housing.

Which, naturally, leads us to consideration of the construction business.

Construction

Unlike many other job markets, the construction trades will probably benefit greatly from the warming. It will be among the hottest of all employment segments. Not only will new dwelling spaces be needed for north-bound migrants, but there will also be many trillions of dollars' worth of work—on an ongoing basis—required to repair and rebuild homes, buildings and infrastructure damaged by the ever-increasing catastrophic weather, wildfires and flooding.

And, of course, we're talking about construction broadly—road, bridge and tunnel rebuilding, repair of powerlines, wind turbine and solar installation and repair, pipelines, airports, ports, railroad rights of way, sea walls and levees. The list of job descriptions of skilled workers required to meet these needs would include carpenters, metal workers, electricians, plumbers, heating and air conditioning specialists, masons, heavy equipment operators and more.

Agriculture

Agricultural employment, on the other hand, will suffer significant disruption. By 2050, much farm and grazing land will have been lost to flooding, increasing heat and drought in many areas of the country. Many farm workers will either need to retrain for other jobs or move to still-productive areas and vie for available jobs.

The agricultural downturn will not only affect farm workers. Reduced output and the increasing cost of fuel will adversely affect the transportation industry—the trucks and trains need to get produce and products to the market. For reasons of transportation costs, most markets will try to rely as much as possible on locally produced agricultural products. Viable farms close to large markets will benefit.

Teaching

Another job segment that will suffer from less demand is teaching, in this case as a result of the falling birthrate. There are currently about 10 million teachers in K-12, college and university.

The U.S. birthrate in 2019 fell to its lowest level in 35 years, well below the requisite 2.1 babies per woman required to sustain our population through birth alone. Researchers expect this trend to continue.

"What we learned from the Great Recession is that every one percentage point increase in the unemployment rate reduces births by one percent," according to Wellesley College Economics Professor Phil Levine.

His research implies there will likely be a COVID baby bust instead of a baby boom in the U.S. That will mean fewer American-born workers and consumers, which could slow long-term economic growth and eventually further reduce the need for teachers.

Diaper Manufacturers Take Note

A new Pew Research Center survey finds that a rising share of U.S. adults who are not already parents say they are unlikely ever to have children. Their reasons range from just not wanting to have kids to concerns about climate change and the environment.

Some 44 percent of non-parents ages 18 to 49 say it is not too likely—or not at all likely—they will have children, an increase of seven percent from the 37 percent who said the same in a 2018 survey. Meanwhile, 74 percent of adults younger than 50 who are already parents say they are unlikely to have more kids, a statistic virtually unchanged since 2018.

Generally, demographers have found that significant social and economic disruptions result in reduced birthrates. The warming certainly meets those criteria.

Manufacturing

Then there's the enormous and diverse manufacturing segment that employed an estimated 13 million workers in 2023, making it the fifth largest employment sector.

Manufacturing employment reached its highest in the U.S. in 1985 at about 20 million. The slow but steady decline in jobs can be attributed to manufacturing moving offshore and the impact of automation. There were significant employment dips in 2010

(11.5 million) and 2020 (11.6) million demonstrating the impact of a recession and COVID.

The health of the manufacturing sector, in large part, relies on two basic factors—the efficiency of the supply chain and consumer demand. As COVID recently demonstrated, these two factors can have a significant negative impact on employment. Well documented COVID-related supply chain disruptions and flagging consumer demand resulted in the loss of an estimated 570,000 manufacturing jobs in 2020, according to the *Monthly Labor Review*.

In the medium term, the impact of COVID on manufacturing—on the economy in general—will pale in comparison to the economic and supply chain disruptions to be caused by the warming.

So, What's a Supply Chain?

"Supply chain" rolls easily off the tongue, masking, perhaps, the extremely complicated—and easily disrupted—process to which it refers. Thus, if "supply chain" is going to be responsible for many of our warming-related economic problems, it's worth taking a closer look at what we're dealing with:

- A supply chain is a network of companies and people that are involved in the production and delivery of a product or service.
- The components of a supply chain include producers, vendors, warehouses, transportation companies, distribution centers and retailers.
- The functions of a supply chain include product development, marketing, operations, distribution, finance and customer service.
- Today, many supply chains are global in scale.
- Effective supply chain management results in lower costs and a faster production cycle.

A supply chain should not be viewed as linear—a literal chain. A better analogy would be a spider web with strands radiating from the center. The number of strands depends on the complexity of the product being manufactured and how many suppliers—sometimes called vendors or partners—are needed to supply components.

Bottom line: Any hiccough in the process can wreak havoc on the manufacture and delivery of goods, reduce supply and result in the shortages and high inflation that, inevitably, will accompany the warming. Permanent or temporary loss of jobs is also a result of supply chain disruption.

Before considering two large consumer-facing employment segments, it's probably a good idea to revisit our old economic friends—inflation, supply and demand and discretionary income.

The impact on the economy of the COVID pandemic is very instructive and provides clues as to what we can expect from the warming. Supply chain issues slowed the manufacture and delivery of consumer products. Fewer products led to higher prices; job layoffs reduced discretionary income. This trifecta led to a spike in inflation and a general economic slowdown.

There is little doubt that the warming will replicate the COVID scenario, but, unlike the pandemic, it will be a permanent and ever-worsening economic nightmare that will likely lead to higher levels of inflation than we have seen, significant job loss and greatly reduced discretionary income.

With that reminder, let's look at the retail and hospitality and leisure segments.

Retail

The retail sector is the largest employer in the U.S. with an estimated 52 million employees. Retailing includes the sale of products and merchandise from a store, by mail or online.

There were about one million brick-and-mortar establishments in the U.S. in 2020 ranging from the "Moms and Pops" to the "Big Boxes." Meanwhile, 13 percent of total retail sales came through e-commerce, primarily the 800-pound gorilla in the market—Amazon. Sales of the gigantic e-tailor account for $302 billion of the $4.4 trillion in annual U.S. retail sales. And e-tail is rapidly on the rise.

Financially, and in terms of long-term employment prospects, retail is the most fragile and least attractive of all employment sectors. In the rough and tumble world of retail, profit margins are razor thin.

It's a Long Wait 'til Black Friday

"Black Friday" is a colloquial term for the Friday after Thanksgiving. It traditionally marks the start of the Christmas shopping season and, as any good consumer knows, many stores offer highly promoted sales at discounted prices and often open early, sometimes as early as midnight or even on Thanksgiving Day. Some stores' sales continue to Cyber Monday or Cyber Week. Generally, it is thought that Black Friday is the beginning of the period when retailers are no longer be "in the red" and finally begin to see profits.

In sum, in terms of employment prospects, get thee as far away from retail as possible. The only exception to this cautionary note is retailing that focuses on consumer needs as opposed to wants—grocery outlets, for example. You may remember the discussion earlier about needs and wants. In the world of the warming—most consumers will have limited discretionary income because of inflation and unemployment. Their focus will be on meeting needs—hamburger, not Nikes.

Hospitality and Leisure

Hospitality and Leisure is the largest subsection within the service industry and is comprised of four main areas—food and beverage, travel and tourism, lodging and recreation. As examples: The food and beverage category includes restaurants and bars; travel and tourism covers various forms of transportation and travel agencies;

lodging varies from hotels and resorts to motels and hostels; recreation refers to leisure activities such as sports, wellness and entertainment.

Over 15 million in the U.S. are said to be employed in this large and diverse industry. But, because of its diversity, it's difficult to estimate the total annual revenue generated.

The segment, however, will suffer the same gradual decline in revenue and employment as retail as the warming heats up. Restaurants, vacations and leisure activities rely on the availability of discretionary income. Thus, medium to long-term employment prospects in this segment are not good.

Restaurant meals provide a good example, tied as they are to rising food prices and the need to increase salaries in order to compete for workers.

No, I Think We'll Eat In Tonight!

Between 2003 and 2023 food experienced an average inflation rate of 2.91 percent per year. In other words, food costing $20 in the year 2003 would cost $35.46 in 2023 for an equivalent purchase. So, food for a $20 meal at your favorite restaurant 10 years ago would cost over $35 today.

Also, restaurant workers are finally seeing improved wages. More than half of U.S. states hiked their minimum wages in 2023, but some restaurant workers could see even bigger gains. California's state minimum wage rose to $20 an hour in 2024.

While no one should begrudge restaurant workers a decent wage, rising costs of food and labor passed along to customers will certainly reduce the appetites of many for a restaurant meal.

Two job categories that will probably grow along with the effects of the warming are Healthcare and Law Enforcement. Employment opportunities in these two categories will be discussed in Chapters 13 and 14 respectively.

If you have plowed through this admittedly quick overview of employment prospects in the coming world of the warming, I think I owe you some sort of summary.

Earlier I suggested that perhaps the most important decision you might make to help you and yours survive the warming is where you choose to live. Your choice of employment is probably just as important.

If just starting out, think carefully about your future employment. If you are already pretty well settled in a job or career that could survive the coming employment disruptions, stay put. If not, you should be thinking about a Plan B.

If you have children, do what you can to point them in the direction of employment that will provide some security. And impress upon them the need to do the same for their children. Don't forget that surviving the warming needs to be a multi-generational effort.

And here's where I make a final pitch for bartering. It may be decades before inflation runs amok and makes currency of less utility. Remember the example mentioned earlier of a loaf of bread costing a wheelbarrow-full of currency in hyperinflated economies?

What Will You Have to Barter?

There is already an active bartering culture in the U.S. Person-to-person bartering is done today through swap meets and online via sites like Craigslist. And don't forget that labor can be bartered. There also are sophisticated barter exchanges located throughout the country—more than 1,100 at this writing—that enable people and businesses alike to use "barter bucks" to trade goods or services for credit that they can apply to something else on the exchange. But, as the warming gathers speed, it will probably be a good idea to develop a network of bartering partners with whom to exchange on a regular basis.

Chapter Thirteen
Staying Healthy in a Warming World

"America's Health Care System is in crisis precisely because we systematically neglect wellness and prevention."
—Tom Harkin, former U.S. Senator

America is a sick country.

Let the numbers speak for themselves:

- The U.S. was once a health care leader in the world. It now ranks 27th, according to a recent study by the World Health Organization. This represents a significant decline from 1990, when it ranked sixth.

- Life expectancy in the U.S. is dropping. We are 46th behind Albania. The average American male can expect to live 74.5 years; the average female, 80.2. According to this 2020 data, Hong Kong leads the world—82.9/88.

- Meanwhile the U.S. is 54th in infant mortality—tied with Serbia. *That, of course, means an American woman is safer having her baby in 53 other countries.*

- Key findings of a 2021 Commonwealth Fund study place the U.S. as last among 11 peer countries in health care. The top-performing countries overall were Norway, the Netherlands and Australia. *We rank last overall despite spending far more of our gross domestic product on health care.* The U.S. ranked last on access to care, administrative efficiency, equity, health care outcomes, and second on measures of care process. *The U.S. was the only one of the 11 countries surveyed not to have universal health insurance coverage.*

Our Shortcomings

According to the Commonwealth Study, four features distinguish top performing countries from the United States: They provide for universal coverage and remove cost barriers; they invest in primary care systems to ensure that high-value services are equitably available in all communities to all people; they reduce administrative burdens that divert time, efforts, and spending from health improvement efforts; and they invest in social services, especially for children and working-age adults.

"In no other country does income inequality so profoundly limit access to care as it does here," David Blumenthal, Commonwealth Fund president, said. "Far too many people cannot afford the care they need and far too many are uninsured, especially compared to other wealthy nations."

Nearly 30 million Americans, nine million of them children, do not have health insurance.

- Americans suffer higher death rates from smoking, obesity, homicides, opioid overdoses, suicides, road accidents and infant deaths than people in other rich countries. In addition, deeper poverty and less access to health care mean Americans with lower incomes die at younger ages than poor people in peer countries. This is according to *Our World in Data* (2020).

- Nationally, 42 percent of adults are obese. Black adults had the highest level of adult obesity at 49.9 percent. Hispanic adults had an obesity rate of 45.6 percent. White adults had an obesity rate of 41.4 percent. Obesity and poor nutrition are not limited to low-income Americans. The prevalence of obesity in the U.S. population as a whole, as indicated, is 42 percent. According to a 2016 listing, America is the 12th most obese country in the world. The first other so-called developed nation to appear on the list is Canada at number 26.

- Obesity costs the United States about $150 billion a year, or almost 10 percent of the national medical budget. It should come as no surprise that Americans lead the world in daily caloric consumption, averaging about 3,500.

Then There's COVID

As is widely known, the U.S., with only four percent of the world's population, has suffered 17 percent of the COVID deaths. As of this writing, 1.2 million Americans have succumbed to the virus. You can put this in better perspective if you go to your road atlas and put crosses through San Jose, California, or Austin, Texas. Each city has about a million population.

Why the abysmal performance? It wasn't that our health care workers didn't work hard enough. The problem was criminal mismanagement at the Federal level. "It's the States' problem," President Trump said. Then there was his politicization of COVID to play to his anti-science, anti-vax base. Is the American public going to be any better served as we face the deepening and diverse health-related effects of the warming?

Unfortunately, the warming is going to make America even sicker.

The climatic conditions the warming is bringing will be responsible for a multitude of new health hazards and an increase in the prevalence and severity of already existing conditions.

The Environmental Protection Agency sums it up: The health

effects of climate change include increased respiratory and heart diseases, pest-related diseases like Lyme and West Nile Virus, water and food-related illnesses, injuries and deaths. Climate change has also been linked to increases in violent crime and overall poor mental health.

The list of ills is long and nasty.

- Increasing temperatures mean more air pollution that will increase ground-level ozone and particulate matter thus leading to diminished lung function and asthma. Higher temperatures also mean longer pollen seasons and more pollen, further affecting asthmatics and even creating new asthma sufferers.

- Extreme heat events have long threatened public health, with many cities suffering dramatic increases in death rates during heat waves. Deaths result from heat stroke and related conditions, but also from cardiovascular disease, respiratory disease and cerebrovascular disease. Heat waves are also associated with increased hospital admissions for cardiovascular, kidney and respiratory disorders. Extreme summer heat is increasing in the United States, and climate projections indicate that extreme heat events will be more frequent and intense in coming decades. (Remember? Phoenix has just appointed the first "Heat Czar" in the country.)

- Heatstroke is a condition caused by your body overheating, usually as a result of prolonged exposure or physical exertion in high temperatures. This most serious form of heat injury can occur if your body temperature rises to 104°F (40°C) or higher.

- Increasing heat alone isn't the only contributor to heat-related discomfort. A new climate analysis explains how, when humidity and heat collide, they create "wet bulb" temperatures that will disrupt daily existence. When heat meets excessive humidity, the body can no longer cool itself by sweating. High wet bulb temperatures make it dangerous to work and play outdoors. As wet bulb temperatures increase, so does the risk of heat stroke—and even death.

- Over the last five years, weather-related deaths are up 35 percent. In 2021, 61,105 weather events resulted in 974 deaths and 1,667 injuries. Winter weather, heat and floods were responsible for the most deaths during 2021.

- In addition to the dangerous flooding that comes with extreme precipitation events, other hazards often appear once a storm has passed. Elevated waterborne disease outbreaks in the weeks following heavy rainfall are not uncommon. Water intrusion into buildings can result in mold contamination that manifests later, leading to serious health risks. People living in damp indoor environments experience increases in asthma and other upper respiratory tract symptoms, such as coughing and wheezing, as well as lower respiratory tract infections such as pneumonia.

Ever Heard of Mast Cell Activation Syndrome (MCAS)?

Several million Americans suffer from this recently identified ailment and don't know what's troubling them. Many people have overactive immune systems and the condition—accompanied by a wide variety of unpleasant symptoms—results when a trigger puts their immune systems into overdrive, producing excess histamine. In most cases mold toxin is that trigger. Increased mold contamination will increase the prevalence of this disease.

- At the opposite end of precipitation extremes, drought also poses risks to health and safety. Drought conditions may increase the environmental exposure to a broad set of health hazards including wildfires, dust storms, extreme heat events, flash flooding, degraded water quality and reduced quantity.

Dust storms associated with drought conditions contribute to reduced air quality because of particulates associated, for example, with increased incidence of *coccidioidomycosis* (valley fever), a fungal pathogen, in Arizona and California.

- Wildfire smoke contains particulate matter, carbon monoxide, nitrogen oxides, and various volatile organic compounds and can significantly reduce air quality, both locally and in areas downwind of fires.

- North Americans are currently at risk from numerous vector-borne diseases, including Lyme, dengue fever, West Nile virus disease, Rocky Mountain spotted fever, plague and tularemia. Vector-borne pathogens not currently found in the United States, such as chikungunya, Chagas disease, and Rift Valley fever viruses, are also threats as temperatures rise.

Tiktok

The Centers for Disease Control estimates the average number of Lyme cases treated in the United States at 476,000 per year between 2010 and 2018, a substantial increase over the annual average of 329,000 cases documented between 2005 and 2010. The rise in numbers parallels corresponding increases in the geographical distribution of ticks that carry Lyme and other diseases. With increasing heat, tick populations are moving steadily north, and species appearing in different parts of the country are also changing.

In the past 25 years the number of counties in which the black-legged tick, which transmits the Lyme pathogen, has more than doubled. The lone star tick, a vector for ehrlichiosis, once limited largely to the southern United States, is now found all the way up into New England.

- Mental illness is already one of the major causes of suffering in the United States, and extreme weather events can affect mental health in several ways. Following disasters, mental health problems increase, both among people with no history of mental illness, and those already ill. These reactions may be short-lived or, in some cases, long-lasting. For example, research demonstrated high levels of anxiety and post-traumatic stress disorder among people affected by Hurricane Katrina. Loss or damage to homes or livelihood, loss or injury of loved ones frequently lead to depression and anxiety.

Even without suffering loss, many will have a difficult time adjusting to the disruptive new social, economic and political realities imposed by the warming. There will be the need for people to reduce their expectations and accept simplicity, self-reliance and sustainability—as I keep repeating—in how they organize their lives to survive in what will be a very different world. This probably will prove to be difficult and depressing for many.

Health Care Workers Needed!

Obviously, the need for healthcare workers will only grow as the warming increasingly affects the nation's health. But unfortunately, there are shortages in key job categories—particularly nursing.

About 100,000 registered nurses left the workforce during the past two years due to stress, burnout and retirements, and another 900,000 reported an intent to leave by 2027, according to a study by the National Council of State Boards of Nursing (NCBSN). *That's almost one-fifth of today's 4.5 million registered nurses.*

Americans are entering the world of the warming in pretty poor health. And, considering the underperformance of our health care system, the uncertainties surrounding health insurance and the new or additional medical challenges the warming will present, how will we stay healthy?

People will simply have to become more proactive and take their health care into their own hands. As the warming crisis deepens, people will have to become increasingly self-reliant when it comes to tending to their health and the health of others for whom they feel responsible.

Since we're taking the long view—a multi-generational approach—someone (the Family Warming Coach?) will need to promote this idea and act as a role model—whether simply to a spouse/partner or a slew of kids and grandkids.

The first thing you'd need to do is clean up your own act. In other words, get as healthy as you can now! This would, of course, require different things—sacrifices—from different people. For example:

- Do you have any "bad" health habits you could get rid of? Or at least curtail?

- How's your weight? Check the charts and, if you need to, work to get your weight as close as possible to where it should be. No fancy fad diets needed. The Food and Drug Administration (FDA) diet is a good place to start. A good target for men is 1,800 calories a day; 1,200 for women. That plus exercise helps take off the pounds.

- Do you have a regular workout routine? If not, find some way to exercise on a daily basis. It need not be pumping iron at a health club or investing in a lot of exercise equipment. Simple aerobic exercises, one or two-mile walks a couple of times a week, regular bike rides or swimming at the neighborhood Y would do.

- Keep ahead of your health with regular preventative check-ups and encourage others to do so.

Become Your Own Medical Advocate and Advocate for Others

Don't simply assume that you and your family are going to receive the medical care you need. Numerous books on medical advocacy are available including: *Trust Your Doctor, But Not That Much!* by Reina Weiner (2017); and *5 S.T.E.P.S. to Being Your Own Patient Advocate* by Dr. Christy Kessler (2013).

To help you do any necessary research, there are a number of detailed medical encyclopedias for home use including the *Mayo Clinic Family Health Book, 5th Ed: Completely Revised and Updated*, by Scott C. Litin.

References such as these would also enable you to take care of diagnosis and treatment of simple medical issues at home. I'm not suggesting you try your hand at an appendectomy. Is it a cold or the flu? How do I dress a wound, deal with an allergic reaction, or splint—at least temporarily—a broken finger?

Another recommendation: Take a first-aid course including CPR.

Becoming familiar with alternatives to conventional medications is also a good idea considering the likelihood that many drugs eventually may be in short supply or become too expensive. A book like: *Herbal Medicine for Beginners: Your Guide to Healing Common Ailments with 35 Medicinal Herbs* by Katja Swift and Ryn Midura (2018), would be a worthwhile addition to a home medical library.

Bottom line: Staying healthy in the world of the warming will require more medical self-reliance than we've been accustomed to.

Chapter Fourteen
Safety and Security In The World of The Warming

"Guns Don't Kill People; People Kill People."
—The National Rifle Association

America is not a safe place.

As we've discussed, we lag behind our peer developed countries in many categories—healthcare, for example. But we stand out in at least two—gun ownership and gun violence.

U.S. civilians own 120.5 firearms per 100 people, the highest rate in the world by a factor of more than two. In other words, we are the only country with more civilian-held guns than citizens. The Switzerland-based *Small Arms Survey* reports that U.S. citizens alone account for 393 million (about 46 percent) of the worldwide total of civilian-held firearms.

Gun violence killed more than 44,000 people in the U.S. in 2022, according to the non-profit *Gun Violence Archive's* records. From 2014 to 2020, gun-related deaths in the U.S. rose 35 percent, as reported the nonpartisan data center, *USAFacts*.

"Most countries do not have anywhere close to the rates of homicides that we do. It's driven principally…because we have decided to make guns readily available to almost anyone, and our interests seem to be more in protecting those who sell weapons and want to own them as opposed to the broader public," according to Daniel Webster, co-director of the Johns Hopkins Center for Gun Violence Solutions.

The *Archive* recorded 656 mass shootings in 2023, an all-time high. Sources differ on the definition of a mass shooting, but CNN and others define it as an incident in which four or more people were shot, not counting the shooter if also victim.

Over 70 percent of mass shootings in developed countries happen in the U.S., according to a 2022 report by the *International Journal of Comparative and Applied Criminal Justice*. "Mass shootings are a uniquely American problem, particularly in relation to other developed countries."

A Firearms Free for All

"Thirty-two states let people carry guns without learning how to shoot one. 'Permitless' carry laws are sweeping the country—and fewer states require gun owners to take live-fire training," according to a *Trace* review.

I would like to have ended this book on a more positive note. But it seems I've saved the worst for last.

Years of research have confirmed what is fairly obvious. Violence and crime increase dramatically in societies that are under stress—whether economic, political, social or as a result of internal strife and discord. The U.S. already suffers from several of these stressors. One has to wonder what the future holds as we face what might be called the mother of all SHTF ("Shit Hits the Fan") events—the warming.

It's my belief that the warming's heat will crack, blister and peel away what has always been the thin veneer of civilization—leading, among other things, to an increase in violence and lawlessness in what is already a violence-prone society.

For safety and security, the populace has depended on its local, county and state police to enforce our laws and to "protect and serve." But as the warming wreaks continuing havoc, law enforcement will find it ever more difficult to maintain the peace. The already "thin blue line" that protects my family and yours from those who would do us harm will, with time, become even thinner.

According to the 2021 International Association of Chiefs of Police Survey on police retention and recruitment:

- 78 percent of agencies reported having difficulty in recruiting qualified candidates.
- 65 percent of agencies reported having too few candidates applying to be law enforcement officers.
- 75 percent of agencies reported that recruiting was more difficult in 2019 than it was in 2014.

"In the wake of the COVID-19 pandemic, a tightening labor market, heightened community frustration with the policing profession, and concerns about officer safety and well-being, law enforcement agencies across the country face an historic crisis in recruiting and retaining qualified candidates."

In a 2022 survey, two thirds of law enforcement professionals stated that police recruitment and retention is their largest issue. *The number of police officers in service has decreased while the population has increased.*

Obviously, Law Enforcement could offer substantial job opportunities as demand in other markets wane.

Let's review a few assumptions about the coming world of the warming:

- Economic and social turmoil will result from continuing climate-related damage to homes, businesses and infrastructure. Eventually the cost to clean up and repair the continuous damage may exceed governmental and personal resources.

- Agriculture will be seriously disrupted by drought and flooding, causing food shortages and high inflation.

- The migration of millions of Americans from the coasts and southern and southwestern climes northward will cause massive housing and employment disruptions.

- Unemployment will increase in many job categories because of diminishing demand.

- The stress of living in this ever-deteriorating environment will greatly increase the incidence of mental illness.

- Traditional law enforcement will not be able to keep up with increasing lawlessness.

What does this suggest about safety and security for Americans? Similar conditions have been seen and are being seen in other countries. Unfortunately, they often result in the breakdown of civil society as evidenced by bloody demonstrations, food riots, looting, an increase in homicide and robbery. In some countries, competition for limited resources has already led to genocide (e.g., Africa's Darfur Region).

Okay, So Who's In Charge Here?

Our founding fathers did us no favors when they failed clearly to delineate the roles of the federal and state governments. Generally speaking, the Constitution leaves all functions to the states not assumed by the Federal Government. This has led to all sorts of mischief during the life of the nation.

The Civil War, or War of Secession—as my 10th grade civics teacher in Virginia insisted on calling it—is, perhaps, not the best example of how the lack of clarity in the document has led to confusion. But the fact that historical and legal scholars continue to this day to haggle over a state's right to secede supports that notion. Actually, the argument was made moot. In Texas v. White (1869), the Supreme Court ruled unilateral secession unconstitutional.

The Supreme Court weighed in on another weighty matter in its

1973 Roe v. Wade decision by granting women access to abortion nationwide. But the Supreme Court giveth and also taketh away. In 2023, the heavily conservative Court reversed Roe v. Wade, placing responsibility for decisions pertaining to women's reproduction rights in the hands of the states. The result has been a patchwork quilt of laws and regulations that has ended up requiring women from "red" states to travel to "blue" states where abortions are still legal. Depending on who's in the White House in 2025, federal law may be used either to reinstate or to ban abortion across the country.

Then, of course, there's the COVID pandemic and President Trump's infamous statement, "It's up to the states!" This led to chaos forcing states to bid against each other for needed equipment and supplies How many lives were lost by trying to push a national problem onto the states is unknown.

Finally, few words about Hurricane Katrina (2005) and the enormous loss of life and damage it caused. The storm flooded 80 percent of New Orleans, killed more than 1,800 and caused $125 billion in property damage. According to a Congressional report, "The storm's damage was greatly exacerbated by the failures of Congress, the Bush administration, the Federal Emergency Management Agency (FEMA), and the Army Corps of Engineers."

Weather forecasters warned about the storm's approach, so accountable agencies should have been prepared. They were not. Katrina exposed major failures in America's disaster preparedness and response systems.

When surveyed, citizens of New Orleans blamed the federal, state and local governments almost equally for the loss life and slow response times

---

Okay, so what's the point?

In the coming world of the warming, people should not expect much help from governments or governmental agencies—at any level. There will be a lack of coordination and confusion, as these examples illustrate, as to who's in charge of what and to whom one should go if help is needed.

The problem? Nobody's planning the adaptation strategies necessary to cope with what's coming—not at the national, state or local levels. The planning and implementation to date continues to focus on reducing greenhouse gas emissions—a worthy goal but, as indicated earlier, one that's too little, too late.

So back to our mantra: "Simplicity, Self-Reliance and Sustainability." At the risk of including a phrase often incorrectly attributed to the Bible: "God helps those who help themselves."

I think at some point Americans will have to rely increasingly on themselves for protection from the growing lawlessness that will accompany the likely collapse of civil society. Depending on your age, you may not be significantly affected. But, if you have children and they have children, it's likely they will be confronted by this warming-related reality as will others in future generations.

This is another reason why I preach *self-reliance* and the need to plan for the warming *multi-generationally*. Part of any planning you, your family and extended family do to prepare for the warming's massive and ongoing disruptions must include considering how to protect yourselves and what you have from those who would take it from you.

How?

There are many factors at play here. For example, where do you live, or would you choose to live if relocation is necessary?

- Single family home in a suburban setting
- A home in a rural setting
- A townhouse or condo complex
- A gated community
- A tightly knit neighborhood
- A multiple-family compound

- A commune (as described in Chapter One of this section)

Obviously, all of these living arrangements pose differing safety and security advantages or disadvantages.

Generally, there should be "strength in numbers." A single-family home in a suburb would be an easier target than a well-secured condo, gated community or communal arrangement in which security is a priority.

Residents of a particularly cohesive urban neighborhood could band together to make mutual security arrangements—an active and well organized 24-hour neighborhood watch, for example.

A home in a rural setting—especially one sitting on acreage of any size—would offer both advantages and disadvantages. Living outside of a heavily populated area means less exposure to urban violence, but without neighbors close by with whom to engage in cooperative security arrangements, a rural home is something of a "sitting duck."

Protection tactics are almost too numerous to list and could be variably adapted to different housing situations:

- An alarm system including CCTV monitors
- High-intensity motion-activated exterior lights
- An intrusion-activated siren
- A safe room in the house
- One or two well-trained watch dogs

And for personal defense:

- Martial arts training
- MACE or pepper spray
- One of any number of varieties of Tasers

Earlier in the book I mentioned the existence of millions of survivalists/preppers who are concerned about protecting their families from any number of SHTF events including civil unrest, natural disasters, nuclear war or erosion of their personal freedoms. For whatever reasons, preppers have the right idea.

But I believe the warming is the mother of all SHTF events. It's actually not an "event" per se. "Event" suggests that there's a beginning and end. *The warming is an ongoing civilization-changing climate calamity. It will require long-term planning and significant lifestyle changes to survive.*

However, the many magazines, websites and blogs produced by the prepper community are valuable resources for information on survival equipment and techniques, the martial arts and weapons, growing food, providing shelter, emergency medical care, etc., and should not be overlooked.

You'll also find many tips and suggestions for planning to deal with short-term natural disasters in case your area is prone to hurricanes, flooding, tornadoes, wildfires. One great idea, in addition to stocking non-perishable food and plenty of water, is the "bug out bag" (BOB) that contains a range of items necessary for survival in case the family has to evacuate.

You may have noticed that there's been no mention of firearms. In potential conflict situations such as these, for most of us, they are probably the first thing that comes to mind. But I believe they deserve special consideration.

First, of course, if firearms are to be part of a protection plan, training is essential. As indicated earlier, as of this writing, 32 states allow residents to conceal carry without any live-fire training. Obviously, this is insane.

But there are also the questions of ethics and empathy that must be considered. *Would you or yours actually shoot someone?* If so, under what circumstances. Depending on laws in your area, what would be the legal ramifications? That's assuming "the law" is still up and running.

I once heard a firearms instructor tell his students that knowing how to shoot a gun is of no value unless, when or if the time comes, you can actually shoot. "Because if you hesitate, show signs of nervousness, your adversary may be able to shoot you first or disarm you."

The vast majority of people are empathetic to varying degrees. The coming world of the warming will bring pain to the empathetic—particularly those with an abundance of empathy. They will be surrounded by increasing numbers of the homeless, hungry and sick as the warming unfolds. They will want to help, but, obviously, the task would be overwhelming.

Often, in each of us, there is a conflict between selflessness and selfishness. But, in the coming world of the warming, self-preservation—the preservation of ourselves and the others important to us—must take precedence.

Perhaps the best one could hope for is the ability to engage in acts of kindness when the occasion permits.

However, the focus will need to be on saving the family, extended family or others who have banded together and planned as best they could to survive. There will likely be violence, bloodshed, death and people in desperate need. But, unfortunately, we may need to sacrifice some of our humanity in order to save it.

EPILOGUE

—Lorin R. Robinson

Earth Day
April 22, 2124

Joss McIntyre sat on his favorite knoll and looked down at The Camp spread below in the steep-walled valley. Though early in spring, the aspens under which he sat were fully leaved, providing welcomed shade against the heat of the bright morning sun.

It'll be 90° plus again today, he thought. The long, hot summers continued to start earlier every year—even at 7,000 feet in the mountains. It had been a few decades since greenhouse gas pollution had slowed. But CO_2 molecules could last up to 90 years in the atmosphere. The warming wouldn't stop any time soon.

The Camp was quiet this morning, a Sunday. A day of rest. He gazed fondly at home. The several dozen cabins, bunkhouse, dining hall, workshop, large barn and outbuildings. Many were made of roughhewn planks taken from the valley's fir and pine.

Crops were in and well along. Corn, soybeans and alfalfa on the terraced hillsides. Vegetable plots. The orchards had already bloomed. Chicks had hatched. Piglets attacked sows' teats. There were calves in the corral. Freshly shorn sheep were in the pasture, fleece already carded and on the looms.

Blades of the two windmills near the barn rotated slowly in the light breeze, turning the generators. Later in the day, if the wind picked up, the connection to the well would be engaged so they could also pump water.

For decades The Camp had solar power. The abandoned panels were on the roof of the barn. By the 2070s, heavy-duty replacement batteries for the system were no longer to be had. The wind generators' limited output was now devoted to operating critical equipment and charging batteries for the short-wave radio, lights and flashlights. The old ones also had enough foresight to stock up on solar-powered landscape lights and floods as well as hand-cranked flashlights—many of which still worked.

Joss opened The Book sitting on his lap. He hadn't looked at it for a while. But something about the day's date—April 22, 2124—struck him as familiar. One of many traditions in The Camp was to keep The Calendar as accurately as possible.

It was Great Great Grampa Mac's journal started when he was about 15. Unlike many of his siblings and cousins, Joss was interested in the story The Book told—how the McIntyres came to this place and the story of the world and what had happened.

He didn't read very well. Few did, though Mac had seen to it that many books were brought up to The Camp. They were all neatly shelved in the dining hall and well-read in the early years. But as time went by, the stories seemed increasingly less relevant. That's where he'd found The Book, dusty and apparently forgotten. The textbooks, on the other hand, were dog-eared. Many had been crudely rebound. The dining hall also served as the schoolhouse.

He opened the journal to page one, and, sure enough, the date of Mac's first entry was April 22, 2024—100 years ago. Next to the date he'd scrawled "Earth Day." Mac had underlined it. And in his cramped hand he'd written: "What a joke! Won't do any good!"

Even as a teenager, Mac had seen through lies about the climate foisted on the public by the fossil-fuel industries. The world's politicians, often in cahoots with the polluters, were unwilling or unable to end our destructive love affair with fossil fuels.

Mac had believed climate scientists who predicted the warming would be a civilization changer. He decided to devote his life to three things—making as much money as he could, raising a family and finding someplace they and future generations of McIntyres would be safe.

For money he learned the building trades and became a wealthy commercial builder. For a wife he took Maggie O'Rourke, a fiery Irish redhead. Together they raised an adventurous brood of three sons and tomboy daughter. For safety Mac found and bought a well-watered and secluded valley high in the mountains well away from civilization. And, over a decade, he built The Camp, the future home of Clan McIntyre.

The Clan—which also included aunts, uncles and cousins—would vacation and work at The Camp until Mac judged it was "time to cut the cord" and disappear, as he wrote in The Book on April 22, 2057. The date was probably not an accident—just another example of Mac's sense of humor.

His entry on that date:

"The economy is in shambles. Government at all levels losing control. Unemployment spiraling. Riots over food. Coastal cities flooding. Countries collapsing. Strong countries overrunning weak. Genocides. Millions worldwide on the move."

By then there were additional McIntyres. Sons had married. There were youngsters. The tomboy daughter, Nancy, remained single. She had studied nursing and became The Camp's healer, passing her skills along to those who would follow.

The first job was to hide The Camp. The construction road into the valley through its narrow opening was erased and replaced by a challenging and carefully camouflaged trail. Then, with all the ingredients on hand, the extended family "disappeared" and began the long and arduous task of making The Camp self-sustaining.

Joss riffled through the pages:

June 3, 2059: "Grandson Jake went walkabout to find a wife. Necessary, but risky, considering what's going on out there. But we must expand our gene pool...."

Mac had been very definite on this point. He wrote: "We don't want to turn into a bunch of hillbillies like the Hatfields and McCoys." This comment took Joss to the encyclopedia in the library and led to information about the dangers of inbreeding.

January 21, 2062: "The West Antarctic ice sheet has collapsed. Greenland is almost denuded. Coastal flooding increasing exponentially."

June 29, 2063: "Grandson Ben returned from walkabout with bad news. He went to the Carpenter place in the next valley where Jake had visited four years ago and brought back Jeannie. It had been destroyed, burned to the ground—marauders. He went on to the Jensen's on the other side of the mountain and hooked up with Maryanne."

February 26, 2066: "Massive blizzard. Heavy snow and wind for three days. Barn roof partially collapsed killing some livestock. Windmills lost vanes. Some cabins ran short of firewood. Had to pry off and burn interior wood."

October 8, 2073: "All communications finally pretty well shut down—Internet, satellite TV, cell phone, commercial radio. Hard to know anymore what's happening in the world. We keep in touch with 'neighbors' by short-wave. Have found several other survivor communities within 50 miles. We hear from a few others at greater distance, but often in languages we can't understand."

July 2, 2075: "A couple of young men came calling today to try to woo away two of our girls."

"Walkabout." Soon it will be my turn, Joss thought. People wondered where Mac got the word. If he ever told anyone, there's no record.

The need to walkabout angered and frustrated Joss. He knew the woman he wanted. He and Emma had played together since they were infants. As they grew, friendship turned into something else. But each knew that a union was impossible. They were first cousins. They had talked about leaving The Camp and striking out on their own. But—to what he was certain he would always regret—head prevailed over heart.

The McIntyre boys go looking for mates when they're about 18. If successful, they leave the bunkhouse and, with help, build a new cabin. Most of the boys succeeded over the generations. A few did not and either went out again or accepted bachelorhood.

One never returned. Somewhere in The Book was an early entry about Grandson Robert. After about a year, they gave up hope and put up a marker, the first in what would become the cemetery in a grove down by the stream.

Mac wore his kilts of McIntyre blue, green and red tartan. He played The Clan theme on the pipes—"We Will Take the Good Old Way." The tune echoed off the valley walls making it sound like a cathedral.

That became the tradition as the graveyard slowly filled. Still, despite some deaths at childbirth, from the flu-like contagion in '68 and natural causes, The Camp continued to grow. Nancy and the healers who followed did their jobs, substituting natural remedies when the pharmacy was depleted of "modern" medicine.

Joss wasn't too worried about his walkabout. It had been much more dangerous in Robert's time. Civilization had fallen apart. Gangs of marauders then roamed the countryside, preying on those who were trying to survive.

In one of his more thoughtful passages, Mac had written: "The warming's heat has cracked, blistered and peeled away what has always been the thin veneer of civilization."

By now most believed that those who could survive had survived. Still, Joss had an occasional nightmare about being caught by marauders. The rule was never to reveal the location of The Camp. Your choices were to escape or accept certain death.

Security had always been a concern. Mac had seen to it that The Camp was liberally supplied with weapons—AR-15s, pump-action shotguns, grenades, night vision gear, Kevlar vests. All adults had to be fully trained and a small group of residents served as a militia that trained more intensely and would serve as the vanguard in any action.

A carefully concealed lookout was carved into the side of the valley's narrow entrance. In the early days volunteers—who called themselves "the watchdogs"—were on duty 24/7. Later, as the threat subsided, watchdogs were on lookout only during daylight hours—on the assumption that the tortuous terrain made a nighttime attack highly unlikely.

But still all had to become competent with the firearms. The militia held monthly drills. Some of the better shots also hunted in the surrounding area. Mule deer were quite common.

In The Book, Mac had written that, despite the potential danger, he did not want The Camp to become too militarized.

"The last thing I want to do is kill another human being," he wrote. "But, if it's us or them, my conscience would be clear."

Joss heard a familiar buzzing. A bee landed on The Book and began an intricate dance that Joss knew meant something in bee language.

"Hey girl," he said. "You've been busy," referring to the pollen collected on her rear legs.

Joss was The Camp's beekeeper, a skill passed on to him by his father. At the other end of the valley were arrayed the 20 hives he maintained. The honey he harvested was the only sweetener available. The bees were also important as pollinators.

The amber-colored liquid also served as a commodity useful in bartering when the occasional visitors arrived. In addition, since the lexicon off affection hadn't changed much over the generations, the boys took honey on their walkabouts. The sweet gesture was understood and appreciated.

He could barely make out the hives clustered in the shade beyond the pond. He heard more than saw some of the kids splashing in the pond that, in fun, had been christened "Loch Ness" when formed by damming the stream running through the valley.

The stream, which had flowed vigorously year around, now became only a trickle in the hot months because of decreasing precipitation and reduced snowpack in the mountains above. Mac had wished he'd thought to dam the stream at the very beginning and install a small hydro-electric generator. But that, it seems, was about the only thing he hadn't thought of.

The pond provided a welcoming place to cool off on summer days when the temperature often exceeded 100°. It was also stocked with fat brown trout.

On some cooler nights, picknickers would make the trek up to Wizard's Nob, the high point above the valley. Mac named the strange outcrop after a fantasy video game character from his youth. From that vantage point, the valley spread for miles as the alluvial plain it was. Low hills stretched along the horizon. Sunsets occasionally could be spectacular.

In recent years, hikers returning after dark reported seeing more and more faint lights spread widely on the plain, flickering in the haze. New neighbors.

From weather records that had been carefully kept over the years, it appeared that temperatures in the valley were leveling off, perhaps reflecting the gradual reduction of greenhouse gases as fossil fuel burning declined with civilization.

Still efforts to escape the summer's scorching heat had become something of an obsession. Early on, some boys out exploring found the small opening to a cave part way up the south, shady side of the valley. The entrance smelled strongly of bear, but they knew the bears were well past hibernation and out and about. So, they pulled away the brush, loose rocks and crawled in.

Later exploration found the cave to be deep and cool with pools formed by water dripping from stalactites. The opening was enlarged, and a heavy door mortared in. The cave became both a favored place to cool off and to store fruit and root vegetables in the winter months.

And some campers had been excited to find evidence of ancient human habitation—arrowheads, charred bones and faint petroglyphs.

Joss thumbed ahead to the last passages in The Book. Mac died in 2086 at 79. The story goes that he had been in failing health for a few years. His last entries were not only hard to read—his handwriting had become almost illegible—but, instead of routine observations about life in The Camp, they were often thoughtful and a bit enigmatic.

Joss had taken time to decipher them. The last entry was two days before he passed.

February 17, 2086: "Why do we call the Earth our 'mother'? That might make people think 'she' cares about us. But does she even know we exist? Did she feel us scraping off layers of her soil, drilling holes deep into her body? Did she know that we were releasing trillions of tons of greenhouse gases into her atmosphere, that we were fouling and acidifying her oceans, burning millions of acres of her forests, sending radioactive mushroom clouds into her skies? Does she know that her temperature has been climbing, her oceans rising, her surface being battered by ferocious storms?

"Of course not. If 'Mother Earth' were aware, she'd be amused that the slightly annoying vermin infesting her body were in the process of self-destructing, saving her the trouble. But she isn't aware and doesn't care. If or when we go, she will take no notice.

"If we are to survive, we are on our own. And we will survive only if we heed the lessons of our greedy, hedonistic and destructive past."

Joss knew the topic of the weekly after-Sunday-dinner discussion tonight would be the hotly debated question of when the Camp should reenter the world. Most younger campers thought it was high time. Many of the older generation were uncertain, fearing it was too soon and what they might confront, leaving the comfortable confines of home.

Last Sunday Emma spoke for the youngsters. She talked about their need for adventure; the need to break out of the hum-drum existence of The Camp. "It's time to start rebuilding the world," she said.

Mac had left no guidance about if or when The Camp would have served its purpose. But Joss knew the time was coming.

He carefully closed the fragile volume. Maybe, he thought, I should read this entry tonight after dinner. On the 100th anniversary of The Book and of that long-ago "Earth Day," the people need to hear, remember and take Mac's final words to heart.

APPENDIX
Surviving The Warming Discussion Guide

My hope is that this book will encourage conversations about the need to start now to prepare for the warming's inevitable impact. The following discussion guide provides the reader with a summary of key information drawn from the book to help organize discussions about the seriousness of the situation and what can be done to make the best of the difficult times to come. My fear is that the frightening enormity of the monster we've created will lead to a paralyzing fatalism—the belief that nothing can be done to save us from its civilization-changing impact. But, as hundreds of thousands of years of history have shown, humankind can be very flexible and adaptable. Those are the traits that can help us cope with what's to come..

Summary Statement

There is going to be the pressing need to readjust our expectations downward in order to cope with growing limitations imposed by the warming. People will need to accept—even embrace—*simplicity, self-reliance and sustainability* in how they organize their lives to survive in what will be a very different world. This will need to be a multi-generational effort.

Why Should We Worry?

There are those who would have us believe that there's still time to reduce greenhouse gas emissions enough to save us from the worst the warming has to offer. The data indicates otherwise.

- Instead of reducing greenhouse emissions—all efforts to the contrary—they continue to increase. Total emissions of CO_2 alone were 37 billion tons in 2023 and are forecast to increase to 37.5 in 2024. Less than 30 percent of the world's energy today is provided by alternative non-fossil fuels—solar, wind, nuclear, hydro, thermal and tidal.

- The parts-per-million (ppm) concentration of CO_2 in the atmosphere now exceeds the 425, well beyond the "tipping point" after which the adverse effects of the warming cannot be avoided. The last time the concentration of CO_2 reached 400+ ppm—some 3-4 million years ago—horses and camels lived in the high Arctic. Seas were at least 30-feet higher, and the planet was an average of 3.6-6.2° (2-4°C) warmer.

- The consensus among climate scientists is that we need to keep the average global temperature increase to 2.7°F (1.5°C) above the 1900 baseline to blunt effects of the warming. At the current rate of greenhouse gas emissions, we will surpass that temperature around 2037. The worst-case scenario for 2100 is a 9.7°F (6°C) average increase.

- Earth's global average surface temperature increase in 2023 was the highest on record. Continuing the planet's long-term warming trend, the year's globally averaged temperature was 2.12°F (1.2°C) above the 20th-century average of 57.0°F (14°C).

- The CO_2 molecule is very robust and may take up to 90 years to dissolve. A molecule that enters the atmosphere today could help Earth continue to warm into the next century.

- At the peak of the 2012 drought in the U.S.—the most extensive since the 1930s—an astounding 81 percent of the country was ranked as under at least abnormally dry conditions. Continued drought will imperil the food supply, greatly increasing costs.

- The worst-case scenario presented for sea-level rise by 2100 is 8.2 feet. Since 1900, the oceans have risen about one foot but are rising at an accelerating pace with a three-foot rise not out of the question by 2050.

- Worldwide, the U.S. is fifth on the list of countries most affected by hurricanes. In a typical year, the U.S. has 12 named storms, six of them hurricanes. Three of these are ranked as major. The number one year for damages is 2017—an estimated $278 billion.

- Over five million acres burned in wildfires fires in 2021—the worst year on record. That's almost the equivalent of the total land mass of New Hampshire.

- There is a huge amount of carbon stored in permafrost in the Arctic and Siberian tundra. The Earth's atmosphere now contains about 850 gigatons of carbon. (A gigaton is one billion tons.) There are an estimated 1,400 gigatons of carbon frozen in the rapidly melting tundra. The irony is that human efforts to reduce the output of greenhouse gases are likely to be offset by this warming-induced outgassing.

- Called "Global Warming's Evil Twin," ocean acidification is doing to the seas what the warming is doing to the land—gradually making it less habitable, in this case, for marine life. The ocean absorbs about 30 percent of the CO_2 released in the atmosphere. It's estimated that by 2100 the seas will be 150 times more acidic than they are today. Much aquatic life will not have time to adapt resulting in a mass die off over time up and down the food chain.

- Americans have great faith in the ability of science and technology to solve problems confronting humankind. But there will be no last-minute technological silver bullet to save us. *We have had the technology—the availability of six widely-available non-fossil fuel sources of energy available for decades—in one case for over 100 years.* They are solar, wind, nuclear, hydro, thermal and tidal. As of this writing, less than *30 percent of the world's energy* is provided by non-fossil fuels.

What, Then, Can We Do?

- Overall, as indicated, we must become realistic and reduce our expectations in order to accept the warming's growing limitations. The mantra to use in developing viable lifestyles should be "simplicity, self-reliance and sustainability." (Section Two, Chapter One)

- Where is it best to live? This is one of the biggest decisions that must be made. As conditions worsen in the Southern Atlantic States, The Deep South and Desert Southwest, people will begin a slow mass migration to the north to escape increasing heat, humidity, violent hurricanes and flooding or desertification. If you live in any of those regions, think about relocating soon to the Northwest, northern Rocky Mountain States, the northern Upper Midwest or areas to the north or northeast of the Ohio Valley. (Section Two, Chapter Three)

- The warming is going to bring severe economic disruptions. Inflation will increase dramatically as supplies of key products are reduced. It will also cost many Americans their jobs. One solution to high inflation is the use of bartering for goods and services—no money needed. (Section Two, Chapter Five)

- In years to come, access to sufficient supplies of affordable food will become problematic. For tips on how to be as food self-reliant as possible, see Section Two, Chapter Eight.

- Only about one percent of all water on Earth is fresh and suitable for human and animal consumption. It's unevenly distributed around the world—and in the U.S. itself—and the supply is slowly dwindling. For suggestions on how to save water, see Section Two, Chapter Nine.

- The ready and affordable availability of energy to power our homes will become increasingly in jeopardy. For tips on how to keep the lights on and provide heating and cooling see Section Two, Chapter 11.

- Another critical decision is how you choose to make a living. Many categories of employment will suffer substantial reductions—retail, manufacturing, agriculture, hospitality and leisure, teaching and real estate. Less affected will be jobs related to solar energy production, the construction trades, healthcare and law enforcement. If you are in school and thinking about a job, look carefully at what is promising in the long term. If currently employed, try to determine if the long-term prospects are good. If not consider a job/career shift, even if retraining is necessary. (Section Two, Chapter 12).

- America is already a sick country and lags behind all other developed nations in healthcare. The warming will make us even sicker and further stress our already stressed system. For suggestions as to how—in the name of self-reliance—to provide care for yourself, family and extended family now and, particularly, in future generations, see Section Two, Chapter 13.

- America is also a violent country. Over time, many of our institutions—including law enforcement—will be seriously degraded, putting civil society in jeopardy. An important requirement for surviving the warming will be the ability to protect what you have from those who would take it. See Section Two, Chapter 14 for self-protection suggestions.

Valuable Online Resources

https://projects.propublica.org/climate-migration
An excellent series of graphics forecasting coming climates shifts.

It enables users to check conditions in their own counties.

Sea Level Rise and Coastal Flooding Impacts
Check the impact of SLR on locations in the U.S at depths from 1-10 feet in detailed graphic representations. (Type into your browser.)

Made in United States
Troutdale, OR
08/09/2024